THERE IS A SEASON

Other books from Liguori by
Dennis J. Billy

Experiencing God
Fostering a Contemplative Life

Into the Heart of Faith
Ten Steps on the Journey

Plentiful Redemption
An Introduction to Alphonsian Spirituality

Soliloquy Prayer
Unfolding Our Hearts to God

The Way of a Pilgrim
Complete Text and Reader's Guide

THERE IS A SEASON

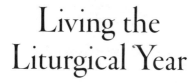

Living the Liturgical Year

DENNIS J. BILLY, C.SS.R.

Liguori
LIGUORI, MISSOURI

Published by Liguori Publications
Liguori, Missouri
www.liguori.org
www.catholicbooksonline.com

Library of Congress Cataloging-in-Publication Data

Billy, Dennis Joseph.
      There is a season : living the liturgical year / Dennis J. Billy.—
1st ed.
            p.   cm.
      Includes bibliographical references.
      ISBN 0-7648-0785-4 (pbk.)
      1. Church year meditations. 2. Catholic Church—Prayer-
books and devotions—English. I. Title.

BX2170.C55 2001
263'.9—dc21   2001029691

Printed in the United States of America
05 04 03 02 01   5 4 3 2 1
First edition

In memory of
Emanuela Messina
"Aunt Millie"
(1904–1995),
Who gave up her life
So that others
Might have a life.

"On all days and seasons…
some marks of the divine goodness are set,
and no part of the year is destitute of
sacred mysteries."
LEO THE GREAT (C. 400–61)

CONTENTS

ACKNOWLEDGMENTS

All scriptural references come from *The New American Bible* (New York: Catholic Book Publishing, Co., 1970). Chapter one was published previously as "Waiting for God: Advent Longing," *Review for Religious* 58 (1999): 566–76. Chapter five was published previously as "Proclaiming the Easter Message: The Relevance of the Resurrection," *The Priest* 57 (no. 4, 2001): 13–20.

INTRODUCTION

H ow do Advent, Christmas, Ordinary Time, Lent, and Easter connect with a person's spiritual life? For some people, the Church's liturgical seasons have everything in the world to do with their walk of faith; for others, these seasons have little relevance; still others may be uncertain about their spiritual meaning. If that is not enough, what makes sense to someone at one point in time may fail to do so at a later date. To complicate matters, the responses to this question can be classified as experiential (rooted in our actual experience of the liturgical year), doctrinal (rooted in what the Church teaches about the liturgical year), or analytical (involved with what scholars have learned about it through study and research).[1]

While all these kinds of responses are worth considering, our focus in this modest book will be on the experiential. We do so for a number of reasons. For one, the teaching of the Church on the liturgical seasons is already well laid out in the (post-)Vatican II documents and in the teaching of the *Catechism*.[2] These, in turn, have been complemented by numerous scholarly studies on the historical development of the liturgical year and its theological significance for the life of the Church.[3] Much less, however, has been written on the impact of the liturgical seasons on our own experience.

In the six chapters that follow, examples from poetry, drama, literature, sacred art, nature, and personal experience will be used to open up the deep spiritual meaning of each season and to uncover its relevance for our everyday lives. In chapter one, Samuel Beckett's *Waiting for Godot* provides a point of departure for presenting the kinds of waiting we can experience during the season of Advent. In chapter two, an icon of the nativity sheds light on the deep symbolic meaning of the Christmas mystery and puts us in touch with the ongoing incarnation of the Word within our hearts. In chapter three, we examine Jesus' hidden life and public ministry to uncover what the call to simple living means for us during the first period of Ordinary Time. In chapter four, personal experience and the insights of Saint Ambrose of Milan bring out the importance of prayer, fasting, almsgiving, and watchfulness for the season of Lent. In chapter five, metaphors of the resurrection found in nature highlight the transformational character of the Easter season. In the final chapter, Michelangelo's fresco, *The Last Judgment,* offers insights into the eschatological character of the second period of Ordinary Time. Our aim here is to offer some general hints about where the seasons of the liturgical year can lead us, if we but take the time to allow their rich and vibrant symbolism to speak to our hearts.

In addition to these guiding literary and visual metaphors, we introduce each chapter with a short poem that reveals something of the spirit of the season in question. These poetic introductions are designed to reflect the dominant imagery and themes of each chapter. Each chapter is also fitted with a spiritual exercise carefully crafted to deepen our understanding of the seasons and help us to discover their specific relevance for our lives. These are intended as points of departure for developing our own insights into the meaning of the season and to help us to enter more deeply into their spirit. Each chapter then concludes with a prayer that celebrates the season under consideration and invites us to raise our minds and hearts to God. Since the liturgical seasons are all about "the Church at prayer," ending the chapters in this way reminds us specifically of our ongoing call to worship.

As far as the general structure of the book is concerned, the chapters themselves treat the various seasons as they occur chronologically during the liturgical year. Because it occupies such a large part of the liturgical year (thirty-four weeks) and is divided into two distinct periods, Ordinary Time is given two separate chapters. This treatment of the material is more in keeping with the experiential sequence of the seasons themselves and allows us to highlight some of the subtle differences that can be found in the one season of Ordinary Time.

This book seeks to raise our awareness of the deep spiritual significance of the liturgical seasons for our lives. We suggest that it be read straight through in closely spaced consecutive readings in order to give the reader a sense of the liturgical year as a whole and how the various seasons fit together in its overall framework. We then suggest that it be read more meditatively during the course of a year by focusing on the appropriate chapter at the beginning of each season. In this way, the reader will be able to savor the meaning of each season as it makes its appearance on the Church's liturgical horizon. To this end, the spiritual exercise at the end of each chapter can be repeated once or twice during the course of a particular season so that the reader can stay in touch with the various themes involved. The same can be said for the prayers that conclude the chapters. During this time, one can also refer back once or several times to the chapter itself so that its themes will remain fresh in one's mind.

The seasons of the liturgical year are all about our journey to God and the transformation of our lives. They seek to change chronological time (that is, *Chronos*) into sacred time (that is, *Kairos*) by steeping us in the mysteries of the Christ event and allowing it to penetrate every dimension of who we are. It is hoped that this little book will foster in us a deeper awareness of the movement of the Christian seasons and help us to appreciate their great significance for our lives today. If we are willing, the pages that follow can help us to delve beneath the surface of the Church's liturgical year and refresh ourselves in its deep, life-giving waters.

THERE IS A SEASON

CHAPTER ONE

WAITING FOR GOD: THE SEASON OF ADVENT LONGING

They watch for Christ
who have a sensitive, eager, apprehensive mind,
who are awake, alive, quick-sighted,
zealous in seeking and honoring Him,
who look out for Him in all that happens, and
who would not be surprised,
who would not be over-agitated or overwhelmed,
if they found that He was coming at once....

This then is to watch:
to be detached from what is present, and
to live in what is unseen;
to live in the thought of Christ as He came once,
and as He will come again;
to desire His second coming, from our affectionate
and grateful remembrance of His first.
JOHN HENRY NEWMAN [1]

S amuel Beckett has written a humorous yet disturbing play entitled *Waiting for Godot*.[2] In it, two scruffy tramps, Vladimir and Estragon, spend their days waiting in a nondescript time and place for someone who never shows up. In this play, Beckett raises questions that go to the heart of the human predicament: the certainty of death, our inability to know what lies beyond it, the struggle we have with belief, our tendency toward skepticism—to name just a few. He provides no answers. He simply raises these concerns and then leaves his audience out in the cold with the rest of his characters: adrift in time and space, impatient and disoriented, and with nothing but their own human warmth to protect them from the harsh realities of life.

Beckett uses the play to set a mirror before our eyes. Most of us do not like what we see. We cannot bear the picture he paints of a life of purposeless waiting, so we close our eyes and try to concentrate on more pleasant, less threatening thoughts—usually to no avail. Beckett has touched a raw nerve within us. He reminds us how difficult it is to find a place for faith in our lives today. He reminds us that all belief in the Western world is now somewhat tainted, tinged by the voices of suspicion and doubt. He forces us to enter the depths of our souls and to leave behind the assurances of our unexamined beliefs.

"Am I waiting for God—or for Godot?"—this is a difficult question for me to ask—and to answer. If I look at the way I actually live my life from one moment to the next, I would honestly have to say, "Probably both," since I experience a mixed bag of faith and doubt, of hope and discontented yearning, of wonder and boredom.

CELEBRATING ADVENT

What does celebrating Advent mean in a world which teaches us, at one and the same time, to believe and not to believe? What does it mean to wait for God in a world that does not stop or wait for anything? What does it mean to expect God's coming when society teaches us time and again not to expect anything from anyone— least of all from God. One answer to these questions might arise from trying to understand what Advent claims to be and then attempting to put our finger on the various kinds of "waiting" people actually experience during this season of the Church year.

The word "advent" comes from the Latin *adventus* and means "coming." As a liturgical season, its traditional purpose is to anticipate the birth of the child Jesus at Christmas. It seeks to do so, however, not as a mere commemoration of a past event, but as a vital sign of all that God sought to accomplish in Jesus' coming as man. As Athanasius of Alexandria once said, "God became human so that humanity could become divine."[3]

Advent looks to the Incarnation as the beginning of the great process of humanity's sanctification. That process begins with the birth of Christ and ends at his Second Coming, when he will bring an end to time and gather all things to himself. Advent anticipates the full range of Christ's redemptive activity. It looks with eager expectation for not one but three comings of Our Lord in our midst: (1) his first coming at Bethlehem, which is recalled by the feast of Christmas; (2) his final coming in glory at the end of time, when he will lead us to his Kingdom; and (3) his continual coming into our hearts, which is the great work of sanctification accomplished through the ongoing historical presence of Christ's Spirit in his body, the Church. The question before us is how can *we*, believing Christians who live in a secularized Western culture, best prepare for these three comings of Our Lord. What is the nature of our longing for these three events? As we celebrate the Advent season, are we waiting for God—or for Godot? Do we really believe that Christ has come, is coming, and will come again? Do we truly long for Christ's coming in the flesh, in our hearts, and at the end of time? Or are we, like Vladimir and Estragon, the two hapless protagonists of Beckett's drama, caught in an endless cycle of aimless waiting?

The true world of Advent longing and expectation is very different from the dreary ennui of Beckett's *Waiting for Godot*. Yet, the two worlds have some things in common: both embrace a way of interpreting reality (one based on faith, the other on doubt); both seek to convince us of the truth about the basis of its beliefs (one is grounded in love; the other in chaos).

To be a believer at the dawn of the twenty-first century is to live in these two worlds. We believe in Bethlehem, but view it through Beckett's mirror. We see the manger from a distance, but somehow suspect it will be empty when we get there, if we ever manage to do so. We say we believe in Christ, but secretly wonder if he is nothing more than a figment of our imagination. We live in two cities, as Augustine would say—the City of God and the City of Man—and both are struggling within us and vying for our attention.

KINDS OF WAITING

Now let us examine what our own experience of Advent longing is really like. We all have a pretty good idea of what it *should* be like. Words like "prayer" and "conversion" come to mind, as well as such phrases as "preparing our hearts" and "waiting for Christ." But what *really* is our experience of Advent waiting in the everyday, nitty-gritty circumstances of our lives? What is it like for those of us who struggle to believe in an age of skepticism, uncertainty, and doubt?

1. For some of us, Advent is a time of *nostalgic regret*. We remember the great joy the season brought us when we were little children, counting the days until Christmas with growing excitement. We cherish that world and the warm memories it brought us. To be honest, we wish we could have it back. The trouble is, we have changed. We have lost contact with the sense of awe and wonder that marked our younger years, and we do not know how to get it back. We have grown up, and some of us are unhappy with what we have become. We look back to

5

the simpler days of our youth and wonder how we could possibly have gotten to where we are now. We celebrate Advent out of an unconscious desire to awaken the child within us. We celebrate Advent out of a sense of nostalgia for the past joy the season has brought us. It reminds us that "unless we change and become like little children, we cannot enter the kingdom of God" (Mt 18:3). As we wait for the birth of the infant Jesus, we hope that somewhere deep within our hearts we will be able to find our own infant selves crying out and in need of human warmth.

2. For some of us, Advent is also a time of *feverish preparation*. There are so many things to do and so little time in which to do them. We can become so busy getting ready for the big feast of Christmas that we have little time for reflecting on its true meaning. There always seems to be one more task to be done: one more ornament to make, one more present to wrap, one more store to visit, one more room to decorate or tree to trim—and so on. Some of us push ourselves to the point of exhaustion. When that happens, one has to wonder if we are not letting the trappings of the feast get in the way of the feast itself. Advent *is* a time for preparing, but it is the way we prepare our hearts for Christ that really matters. We need to welcome Christ by fostering a contemplative attitude toward life and taking time to ponder the mysteries of faith that have given rise to this

great celebration. Otherwise, we run the risk of desacralizing the season of Advent and turning it into nothing more than an extended shopping season for a once religious but now very secular holiday.

3. For some of us, Advent is also a time of *pensive expectancy*. Yes, even in a culture of doubt and uncertainty, Advent can still be a genuine time of wonder and expectation—even for grownups! It still stirs the embers of our hearts and makes them glow with a deep yearning for what we instinctively sense "things should be like." Advent is a time of annunciation. It presents us with the Good News of Jesus Christ in its stark simplicity. It awakens the child within us and asks us to allow that child to get excited about all the gifts he or she will receive as a result of Christ's coming. We hear the message of Advent, and find ourselves wishing to believe it, despite what the conflicting voices within us might be saying. During Advent, the star of Bethlehem arises and then shines in the darkness of our hearts. We wait for it with expectant hope. Waiting, however, is not enough. The question we must ask ourselves during this season is whether we, like the Wise Men from the East, have the vision, the strength, and the courage to follow its lead.

4. For some of us, Advent is also a time of *growing indifference*. We have experienced Advent many

times before in our lives, and do not see it as any-thing particularly special. We are turned off by the rampant consumerism that fills Western society. We do not take Advent seriously because, to our mind, most others do not. To be honest, we have better things to do with our time. "Bahhhh! Humbug!" as the infamous Scrooge would say. Life is hard, exact-ing, and tedious. We are put on this earth to work, not to twiddle our time away with silly ideas that have no impact on the things that really matter. Ad-vent cannot add one second to our life on earth (or take it away, for that matter). Why get caught up in the spirit of an annual celebration that ultimately has very little effect in the way people live their lives? The world will be no different after the celebration of Advent and the Christmas season than before. So why make such a fuss about it?

5. Finally, for some of us, Advent is a time of *lingering loneliness*. Many people hate the holiday season and cannot wait until it is over. This aversion is usually quite personal. It often has to do with a sinking de-pression or state of melancholy that sets in out of a sense of loneliness and dissatisfaction. It should be no surprise to us that the suicide rate takes a sharp turn upward during this holiday season. Many oth-ers do not take such drastic measures, but feel rather lost in their loneliness and yearn for the holidays to pass. They have no family to go home to or, if they do, dysfunctional relationships keep them away or,

at the very least, always on guard. This period of waiting is painful for them. Old memories are stirred and rise to the surface of consciousness. Old battles are fought; old wounds, reopened. The pain of the past makes the present unbearable. Many lose themselves in drink and drugs. They may forget their pain for an hour or two, but it always comes back with a vengeance. When it does, they always feel worse than when they began. Such loneliness may or may not be a stranger to you. We should remember, however, that any of us could one day fall victim to it. There, but for the grace of God, go I.

Nostalgic regret. Feverish preparation. Pensive expectancy. Growing indifference. Lingering loneliness. These are some of the moods that come over us as we celebrate the *adventus* of Christ to the world. Some of these attitudes toward Advent longing may exist in us simultaneously. Others may come and go, rising and sinking in the deep well of our unconscious. We live in a complicated world. We are capable of feeling many emotions on many levels, many of which may even seem to conflict with our most firmly held beliefs. During this Advent season, each of us has to ask himself or herself personally: "Am I waiting for God—or for Godot?" Well, are you? You tell me. Or better yet, why don't you tell yourself? Or better even yet, why don't you tell God?

OUR DEEPEST YEARNINGS

What are we to do with so many types of Advent long-ing? Repress the ones we feel threatened by? Listen only to those that support the traditional point of view? At-tend only to those that make sense to us? All of these longings (and more) exist within us in one way or an-other. Some are quite distinct; others, barely noticeable. Still others vary in degrees of intensity. Such conflict is the price we pay for walking the path of faith in an age of doubt and uncertainty.

But let us ask if there is more here than meets the eye. Does not faith, of its very nature, imply the possi-bility of doubt? If this is so, then is our age really all that different from any other? Were not the voices of suspi-cion, doubt, and unbelief present at the very moment of Christ's birth? Do not the Gospels themselves present the journey of Mary and Joseph to Bethlehem against the backdrop of ignorance, indifference, and hostility? If the faith of Mary and Joseph, her betrothed, was able to survive and even flourish in the midst of such dark and gloomy times, so can ours. What is more, the shiv-ering child who came from Mary's womb on the first Christmas morn was able to draw to himself the won-der of the simple-hearted, the adoration of the wise, and the jubilant hymns of the heavenly host. Believe it or not, he does so even today. Then, as now, the season of Advent celebrates "a light that shines in the darkness, a light that the darkness could not overpower" (Jn 1:5). The only difference for us is that the setting has somehow shifted. If the Gospel narratives projected that darkness onto the outer world, Beckett's mirror (and the world it represents) projects it inwardly to the turbulent world within our hearts.

Centuries after the birth of Christ, even as darkness envelops much of the world we live in, we have the added burden of experiencing that darkness within our own hearts. For this reason, belief is so much more difficult. But it can be achieved, for if Christianity is true (and either it is or it isn't), then Jesus, the Word made flesh and the Light of the world, promises to enlighten our minds and dispel the darkness from our hearts. We cannot cast darkness out of our hearts—but God can. Jesus himself tells us that everything is possible for God (Mk 10:27)—and that makes all the difference.

The season of Advent proclaims our deepest yearnings for oneness with God and affirms that this oneness with God is not only possible, but actually taking place. The season of Advent is full of promise, so much so that some of us are taken aback by its full meaning. Yet, others of us—attached as we are to life in a secularized Western culture—may only be able to say that we would like to believe, that we would like to move forward along the way of "faith seeking understanding." To do this we must humbly admit both our attraction to faith and our lack of it. We who look through Beckett's mirror must also look into the mirror the Gospels place before us. They have everything to do with the birth of Christ in the human heart. Only when we read them as the living story of Christ's presence in our hearts will we be able to

11

recognize the darkness within us and allow the light to accomplish its work in us.

GOD WITH US

Someone once said, "Paradise for God is to dwell in the human heart."[4] This simple phrase has deep scriptural roots (Prov 8:31; Jn 14:23) and goes to the heart of the Advent story. Our longing for God, however feeble and conflicted, pales in comparison to God's infinite and unending longing for us. That longing has existed from all eternity and reached new heights in the person of Jesus Christ who as the Word made flesh, allowed God to experience the human heart from the inside out.

Advent looks forward to the birth of Emmanuel, "God with us." In Christ, God has entered the depths of human experience and promises to transform our own. *He* will take the initiative. *He* will seek us out. *He* will bring light out of the darkness of our hearts and show us which way to walk. That is what he promises to do for us. The work is God's, not our own. For our part, probably the best thing we can do is simply open our hearts and let him do his work in us.

What does that mean for us? As far as our experience of Advent is concerned, there is no need to "make-believe" that the secularized culture around us does not affect "the way we believe." Some of us spend so much time convincing ourselves that we are "true believers" that we do not have time to listen, I mean *really* listen, to the pressing concerns of our own unbelieving hearts.

We waste so much energy putting on a good face for fellow believers that we fail to ponder our faith and put to it the important questions that presently define the existential plight of the Western soul.

What we need to do is to get in touch with our real experiences of Advent longing, those I have enumerated previously—nostalgic regret, feverish preparation, pensive expectancy, growing indifference, lingering loneliness—and any others we can put our finger on. We need to stare them straight in the eye, ponder them and, when the time is right, lift them up with a deep sigh from the heart to God saying, "Lord I believe. Help my unbelief!" (Mk 9:24). We will be victimized by our doubts if we do not express them in faith to God. God, in turn, will not perform the work he wishes to accomplish if we do not let him. And we will not let him in if we insist on maintaining tight control over what we think our experience of Advent *should be like* and never allowing our experience of what it is *really like* to see the light of day. For many of us, our idea of God has become so small, that we somehow think that he would run away in horror if he ever saw what our interior world was really like. We think that the only reason why God wishes to dwell within our hearts is because he does not realize how much darkness and confusion really lurk deep within us. The problem is we are wrong—dead wrong! God knows what we are like through and through, and he still desires to come to us and make his home in us. "Paradise for God *is* to dwell in the human heart."

CONCLUSION

What can we say by way of conclusion? Only this: our Advent longing is possible only because God has all along been anxiously longing for us. It is God who has chosen us (not the other way around). Otherwise, we would be deluding ourselves into thinking that our longing for God in some way justifies his coming—and it most assuredly does not. Christmas is all about God's gift to the world. The season of Advent looks forward to that gift. It celebrates not so much *our* longing for God as it does *God's* longing for us which made the "gift" of Jesus, the Word made flesh, possible.

As such, Christ's three Advent comings appear in an entirely different light. The first, Jesus' coming at Bethlehem, makes possible the second. It allows him to dwell within our hearts and to effect the gradual process of transformation that takes place during our lives and which, for most of us, will continue long after we die. The second, Jesus' birth within our hearts, makes possible the third. That is to say, Christ will usher in the end of time not from without, by displaying his power in some external cataclysmic intervention, but from within, by thoroughly transforming the depths of our hearts and then flowing out from there to usher in the radical transformation of the world.

When seen in this light, we may find ourselves wondering if he ever really came, if Christ really is coming, and if he ever is going to come. We may find ourselves hounded by all sorts of doubts. Such is the plight of faith in the present stage of its journey through time. Let us not get too troubled by the dreary picture our doubts reveal. We want the whole truth, not the partial truth.

What am I getting at? Life is bigger than Beckett's troubling existential mirror. It is bigger than our doubts. It is bigger also than our insufficient Advent longings. The season of Advent itself tells us so. It announces that God, the source of Life, loves us in spite of ourselves, even in spite of our difficulties with faith and our paralyzing suspicions and doubts. It tells us that he yearns to dwell within our hearts and will accept whatever space we give him. He does not ask us to prepare a palatial mansion for him or a strong interior castle (few, if any, are capable of such great feats). He is much too unassuming and humble for that. All we need to do is set up a small little crib for him in some unwanted, darkened corner of our hearts. That will be enough welcome for him. It is all he asks of us, at least for now—to give him a chance to weep and cry, to be warmed, nourished, and loved, to experience paradise in our hearts. The Christmas story is Jesus' story. The season of Advent reminds us that it is also our story. As we wait for his coming, let us remember that he has all along been quietly waiting for us.

Spiritual Exercise

On a sheet of paper list the various kinds of waiting that you go through during the Advent season. Which do you experience the most: nostalgic regret, feverish preparation, pensive expectancy, growing indifference, or lingering loneliness? Which do you experience the least? What combinations of these various types of waiting have you experienced during this season? How would you describe them? Are some days better than others? Continue by drawing up a list of your deepest longings. Ask yourself if they have changed in any way over the years. See if they have changed in any way as this particular Advent season has progressed.

When you feel you have written enough, take some time to reflect upon what you have written. Then take another sheet of paper and write down the kinds of waiting and longing that you would most like to experience during this Advent season. End by asking God to help you to prepare for his coming in a serious and worthy way. If you wish, gather some drawing materials and sketch a picture of what the following phrase might look like: "Paradise for God is to dwell in the human heart."

Prayer

Lord, during this season of Advent longing, I ask you to help me to ready myself for your coming. You entered our world so many years ago to save us from darkness. I ask you to enter the world of my heart and to cast out the darkness that blinds me and leads me astray. Teach me patience, Lord. Help me to wait for your coming. Enable me to put up with the many moods that come over me during this season. Help me to prepare a worthy place for you in my heart. Come to me, Lord. Be born within my heart. May your Word become flesh in me so that my deepest yearnings may reach their fullness in the depths of your love. Be with me, Lord. Never leave me. Help me to reach out to others and to allow myself to be touched by their love. Thank you for your love. Thank you for looking for paradise within my heart. I love you, Lord. Help me to love you more.

Fifteen century, Ambroveneto Collection, Vicenza

AN ICON OF THE NATIVITY OF CHRIST

CHAPTER TWO

RE-CREATING HUMANITY: THE SEASON OF CHRISTMAS JOY

*This is the Month, and this the happy morn
Wherin the Son of Heav'ns eternal King,
Of wedded Maid, and Virgin Mother born,
Our great redemption from above did bring;
For so the holy sages once did sing,
That he our deadly forfeit should release,
And with his Father work us a perpetual peace.*

JOHN MILTON,
"ON THE MORNING OF CHRIST'S NATIVITY"[1]

Christmas is a joyful season, a time when just about everyone, in one way or another, wants to be a little child—even God. This desire may be close to the surface or buried beneath layers of sophisticated "adult" denial. It may show itself in a mixture of emotions—happiness, sadness, anger, loneliness, regret. It may even take physical shape: in the songs we sing, in the food and drink we share, in the gifts we exchange, in the rituals we perform. Whatever it is like, this desire puts us in touch with the essence of the Gospel message: "...whoever does not accept the reign of God like a little child shall not take part in it" (Mk 10:15). At Christmas, Jesus enters our world so that we might become a part of his. Emmanuel, "God with us" comes to us as a helpless child in swaddling clothes. He does this so that we might embrace him, the God of Love and, in doing so, encounter anew our own vulnerability and child-like yearnings.

RE-CREATING THE SCENE

Each year the Christmas story needs to be discovered anew within the human heart. The nativity scene is central to this process of rediscovery. It was Francis of Assisi (1181/82–1226) who first conceived the idea of re-creating the scene of the Jesus' birth. At that time, he used real-life people and animals to convey a dramatic sense of God's humble entrance into the world. Since then, it has become an important expression of the feast's deep, religious significance: "God became human so that humanity might become divine."[2] If these words of Saint Athanasius tell us why the incarnation came about, then Francis's nativity scene provides us with a way of entering into that message and taking it to heart.

Today, most of us follow Francis's example, but have replaced the living characters with small wooden or clay figurines of Mary and Joseph, the ox and ass, the shepherds coming from their fields with their sheep, the astrologers from the East following the star to Bethlehem. Each figure is a symbol that invites the beholder to contemplate the mystery of that small child lying in the manger who, as events unfold, would change the course of history and the movement of the human heart.

The nativity scene has much to teach us. Author Caryll Houselander points out that "the crib showing the nativity in all the cities and villages and Catholic homes of the world is not only there to commemorate Christ's first coming to earth, it is there as a symbol of Christ's birth *in us*."[3] For Christ to be born in us we must be willing to become vulnerable "like little children" and place our complete and utter trust in God. According to Houselander, "Christmas does not only mean that God became man and was born as a human infant on a certain night in Bethlehem, two thousand years ago; it means that, but equally, that because of that, Christ is born in us today."[4] Each of us appropriates the story of Jesus' birth in such a way that it becomes a very personal narrative of the Word becoming flesh in us. Each story (both yours and mine) needs to be meditated upon and shared. Only by doing so will we ever discover its ultimate, transforming significance for our lives.

THE ICON OF THE RE-CREATION

The scene at Christ's birth is a frequent theme in Eastern Christian iconography, where it is often referred to as

"The Feast of the Re-Creation." In the Eastern churches, icons are considered "windows to eternity." They are instruments of prayer intended to give us a subtle glimpse into the beyond. They do so by juxtaposing imagery and symbols in a two-dimensional layout that transfixes our gaze and enlarges our conceptions of time and space. To achieve this effect, the icon in question must be presented in a particular manner according to certain standardized norms. Those icons of the nativity are no exception. They include the same general features with roughly the same cast of scriptural characters as depictions of the nativity in Western art.

In many ways, the icon of the nativity is to the Eastern churches what the Francis's nativity re-creation became for the West: a sacred symbol of the incarnation. The two, of course, share much in common. Both are creative expressions of the artist's imagination. Both are intended as instruments of Christian prayer. Both seek to draw us into the mystery of what took place at the moment of Christ's birth: one, through a three dimensional depiction of the nativity scene: the other, through a carefully designed presentation of pertinent symbols and images. Both borrow heavily from the two major infancy narratives (that is, Matthew and Luke).

These similarities, however, cannot dispel some major differences: In keeping with Francis's original intention, the nativity scenes of the West generally favor a realistic portrayal of the infancy narratives. They focus on the humanity of Christ, the love of the family into which he was born, the wonder of the shepherds, the revelation to the Gentiles, and the adoration of the heavenly host. Although the Eastern icons of the nativity contain many of these emphases, they are much more symbolic in nature and present a wider range of underlying theological motifs. Listed below are the major features represented in the nativity icon along with their relevant interpretation.[5]

1. *The Cave.* In contrast to the Western nativity scenes, which often place the newborn Christ in a man-made structure such as a barn or a stable, Eastern icons center on a cave. Such a natural formation is a powerful symbol that stands for all that is mysterious, dark, and unknown in life. In the context of the nativity, it signifies the darkness of sin and the fallen humanity that Jesus has been sent to redeem. In the icon, the cave appears as a gaping hole in the earth. As God, Jesus enters into the earth; as man, he comes from the earth. The cave symbolizes Jesus' embrace of the human condition and of the sin he has come to help us overcome. It represents all that we do not know about ourselves. It is a foreshadowing of the death he will endure and of the tomb where his body will one day rest. Its central place in the icon reminds us of all the sorrow that lies ahead for this child and of the great price he would have to pay for our redemption.

2. *The Manger.* The Gospels tell us that the infant Jesus was lying in a manger (Lk 2:7). In the icon of the

nativity, this open box or trough that was normally used to hold feed for livestock, holds Jesus, the precious Bread of Life. It is no mere coincidence that it is represented in the shape of an altar. The eucharistic overtones of the scene are clear. Through the offering of his body and blood, Jesus becomes life-giving food for the world. The manger holds this offering and thereby becomes a symbol of the cross from which Jesus hung and of the altar upon which the sacrifice of the Mass would be celebrated in his name. Although the manger was usually made of wood (hence the easy connection with the cross), in the icon it is often depicted as being made of stone (hence its likeness to an altar and, in some cases, even a tomb). In either case, it is made of materials grown, gathered, or hewn from the earth. The manger is the first part of the earth to touch the infant Jesus. It is earth's gift to the God who would redeem its inhabitants and make of it a new creation.

3. *The Swaddling Clothes.* The Gospels also tell us that the infant Jesus was wrapped in swaddling clothes (Lk 2:7). In the icons of the nativity, the infant is wrapped in a winding sheet, the kind one would expect to find around a corpse. Once again, Christ's redemptive death comes to the fore. From the moment of his birth, Jesus is depicted as one who is being prepared for his ultimate sacrifice of self. His mummified appearance reminds us that new life comes to us only at great cost. The cave, the man-

ger, the swaddling clothes all point to Calvary, the ultimate test of the divine self-emptying. Wrapped for burial from the moment of his birth, the infant Jesus cannot escape his fate (even his arms and legs are tightly bound). Only he can enter the darkness of the cave and come out alive—and with the rest of humanity in tow.

4. *The Ox and Ass.* Although they are not specifically referred to in the Gospel infancy narratives, the ox and ass are a fixed feature in all nativity icons. In their typical placement, these representatives of the animal world stand close to the manger and have the privilege of being the closest living creatures to Christ, even closer to him than his mother, Mary. They hold this primacy of place because of their strong biblical reputation: "An ox knows its owner, and an ass, its master's manger; but Israel does not know, my people has not understood" (Isa 1:3). The ox and ass recognize Christ for who he is and peer with wonder into the manger from which they are normally fed. There, they find what human pride refuses to accept: the Word having become flesh in the infant Christ. The ox and ass represent the innocence of all domesticated animals, their devotion to their masters, and their deep earnestness to please. They celebrate the animal dimension of Jesus' human nature and stand in marked contrast to the doubts and suspicions displayed elsewhere on the icon.

5. *Mary and Joseph*. Mary, the virgin mother of the infant, is the largest figure in the icon in order to demonstrate her prominence in terms of the Christmas feast. Cushioned in red, the symbol of chastity, she lies outside the perimeter of the cave to show that she has never been touched by the darkness of sin. She and the cave practically surround the ox and ass, the manger, and the infant Christ. The implication here is that Jesus, the Light of the world, has come out of the darkness of Mary's sinless womb to conquer the darkness present in the world—especially in the human heart. Depending on the icon, Mary is looking at her infant son, at the beholder, or at her bewildered husband. A distraught Joseph is usually found in one of the icon's lower corners. Confusion is on his face and he rests one hand on his cheek to register his dismay. He seems genuinely perplexed by what has just taken place. He struggles to believe in the miracle of the virgin birth, but is hounded by suspicion and doubt. The devil stands before him in the shape of a shepherd and tells him that the virgin birth is simply not possible.

6. *The Magi*. Standing in marked contrast to Joseph's confusion and doubt is the steadfast faith of the astrologers. In the nativity icons, these wise men from the East come on horseback or on foot bearing their gifts of gold, frankincense, and myrrh. The light from the star of Bethlehem points out the cave where the Christ child lies. The movement of this star reminds

us that the whole universe is alert to what is happening in this seemingly God-forsaken corner of the earth. This star is moved by God's providential hand and is often depicted beneath an anthropomorphic representation of the Trinity. The wise men represent the Gentile nations. They have come a long way to pay homage to the newborn king of the Jews. They are of different ages—young, mature, and old—to remind us that God dispenses his wisdom however he pleases, regardless of a person's age or experience in the world. As men of learning, they also remind us that the Gospel message is not contrary to the truths of science. They follow a star and discover the Light of the World. They set out in search of wisdom and kneel at their journey's end before the Incarnate, the Wisdom of God himself.

7. *Shepherds and Angels.* A nativity icon normally includes at least one shepherd. These unsophisticated working men hear the good news of Christ's birth while they are tending their flocks. They receive that message with joy and raise their horns to their lips to spread the news. In addition to shepherds, the icon usually contains a number of angels. These members of the heavenly host represent the world of spirit. They are normally placed higher up on the icon panel and act as messengers of the Lord or servants of praise and adoration. These functions are normally distinguished by the position of their heads and hands: upward, in the case of adoration; down-

ward, when conveying a message. The witness of
the angels strengthens our belief in the miracle of
the incarnation.

8. *The Baptismal Font.* Finally, most icons of the na-
    tivity display the sacrament of baptism in progress
    or about to take place, usually in one of the lower
    corners of the icon. A mother holds her naked child
    in her arms as she watches a minister of the sacra-
    ment fill the baptismal font with water. A sense of
    anticipation permeates the air. The child is about to
    be baptized into the death and resurrection of Jesus
    and turned into a new creation. The birth of Jesus,
    which happened so very long ago, makes this pos-
    sible. On some icons, the bowl of the baptismal font
    is lined in black, a deliberate color pattern linking it
    closely to the darkness of the cave. When seen in
    this light, what happens in the cave of Bethlehem
    occurs also at the baptismal font. Jesus was born
    into the world to cast the darkness out of it. At bap-
    tism, he is born in the human heart to do the same.
    The juxtaposition of historical events, such as the
    nativity of Christ and the ritual of infant baptism,
    captures for the beholder a sense of the eternal in
    the present moment.

PONDERING THE CHRISTMAS STORY

One way of discovering the deep spiritual meaning of
the Christmas story is for us to ponder the theological

significance of the Eastern icons of the nativity. Time allowing (and with appropriate adaptations) the tradition inspired by Saint Francis could be used to similar effect. The sequence of the following reflection corresponds exactly to the order of symbols outlined in the previous section.

1. *The Darkness of Sin.* When we ponder the cave in the icon, we come up against the ugly darkness of sin. The darkness of the cave reminds us of the mysterious, unknown quality of evil in our lives. Just as darkness is an absence of light, so too is sin an absence of good, a "missing of the mark." If we are honest with ourselves, we will eventually admit that we miss the mark on a variety of levels. On a personal level, we know that, at various times in our lives, we have made conscious decisions to hurt ourselves, others, even God. We are responsible for these actions and must one day answer for them. On a societal level, we know that we participate in structures of oppression that denigrate rather than celebrate the dignity of the human person. Rather than working to change these structures, we wallow in indifference and often pretend that such problems do not even exist. On a universal level, we sense that our own humanity is somehow bent out of shape. The "sin of human origins" manifests itself in the unruly passions and desires that flame the fires of jealousy, hatred, greed, and lust in our hearts. Here, the darkness of sin penetrates even our unconscious

lives. We recognize that there is so much that we do not know about ourselves. It would be folly to think that the darkness of the Christmas cave has not entered our hearts, our minds, our conscious, and even our unconscious thoughts.

2. *A New Creation*. The manger, made of materials hewn from the earth, reminds us that Jesus came not only to save humanity but also to create a new heaven and a new earth. The Eucharist gives us a glimpse of what that new creation will be like. The manger cradled the infant Jesus when he first entered our world; we cradle him in our hands when he enters our world during the sacrifice of the Mass. When we ponder the manger, we see the wood of the cross, the altar upon which the Lamb of God was offered up for the sins of the world. When we look at the infant it holds, we need to ask ourselves about the depth of our belief that Jesus' body and blood has become for us "the Bread of Life and the cup of eternal salvation." We need to ask ourselves also if we truly believe that the birth of this child marks the beginning of a new age in the history of the world, one with no place for the darkness of sin and death and one which elevates the earth itself to new heights. The English word "manger" is related to the French word "manger," meaning "to eat." The message of the manger is that the transformation of the world takes place during our sharing in the eucharistic banquet. The transformation of the

bread and wine into the body and blood of Christ is an efficacious sign of the kingdom that is to come.

3. *Jesus' Passion and Death.* In an icon of the nativity, Jesus' swaddling clothes strongly resemble his burial shroud, as if to say that the mystery of his birth can be understood only against the backdrop of his approaching death. From the very beginning, Jesus' passion and death are woven into the fabric of his life. He came into this world only to leave it in one of the most horrible ways imaginable. His suffering and tragic death on the cross enabled him to become an instrument of humanity's rebirth. When we ponder the Christ child in swaddling clothes, we are called to meditate upon the relationship between life and death—for Jesus and for ourselves. Doing so is never easy, since we can always find reasons to do the contrary. In the icon, however, the intimate bond between life and death smacks us right in the face. You and I were born and will one day die. There is no escaping it. Interestingly enough, pondering the end of life helps us to find meaning for the rest it. To ignore death or to pretend it does not exist benefits no one, least of all ourselves. Only by accepting our human mortality can we ever begin to look beyond it. Only then will we appreciate the great gift that God has given in the mystery of the incarnation. Only then will we begin to understand why even the great joy of Christmas is so often tempered by a lingering touch of sadness.

4. *Our Physical Existence.* The ox and ass bid us to contemplate the physical, animal dimension of our nature. As domesticated animals, they remind us that our physical being and bodily passions achieve their fullest expression when they live under the gentle sway of reason's rule. If the latter rebel, they quickly lurch out of control. Wisdom became flesh in Christ and yearns to do so in us. For Christ to be born in us, we must allow every dimension of who we are— the physical, the emotional, the intellectual, the spiritual, and the social—to come under the tutelage of the Word. The ox and ass remind us that even our bodily existence must bow before the cradle of incarnate Wisdom. The physical aspect of who we are embraces also our emotional life, especially our tendency toward anger and inordinate desire. These need to be moderated by virtuous living. When we ponder the animals in the icon and examine the wonder in their eyes as they gaze upon the infant Christ, we are invited to examine our attitudes toward our bodies and to ask ourselves if we are giving them the care they deserve. We are also asked to look at any attitudes or addictions that we may have which denigrate our bodies and repress our emotions. Only when we place our bodily and emotional needs before the Lord will we be able to understand and celebrate our full human dignity.

5. *Faith and Doubt.* When we look at the figures of Mary and Joseph in the icon, we meet the faces of

faith and doubt. These faces are married to one another—and both are saints. The icon puts us in touch with the dynamics of belief. Mary is first and foremost the woman of faith. Graced from birth, her life was a continual "Yes" to God and his will for her. Through her courageous *fiat*, she makes the mystery of the Incarnation possible. She lives continually by the light of faith and has never known the darkness of sin. In some nativity icons, she turns her compassionate gaze not toward her newborn son, but to her struggling husband. In the icon, Joseph is depicted as one beset with confusion and doubt. He believes his wife, but wonders how she could give birth without human intercourse. He struggles with his belief in the incarnate God. He struggles, perhaps most of all, with his own role in the divine plan of redemption. If Mary represents the person of faith we hope one day to become, Joseph represents the kind of believer most of us, in fact, really are. Each is a person of faith (albeit at different stages of maturity). Each wears a halo. Each challenges us to examine our belief in the Christ child. The icon reminds us that our faith is often strengthened by our doubts. It calls us to bring the depths of our faith to the surface of our consciousness and to examine our doubts and be strengthened in the process.

6. *The Journey of Faith*. We overcome our doubts only by undertaking a journey. In the icon, the Magi rep-

resent the journey of faith that each of us are called to embrace. These astrologers from the East set out on the long, harrowing journey to find the secret to be revealed to them by a single light shining in the darkness. That star leads them to the Christ child, to whom they offer their precious gifts. For most of us, life is an exceedingly difficult task. If we wish to arrive at our destination with our faith intact, we need to listen to our hearts and be men and women of conviction. What we discover at the end of our journey is already secretly present at our journey's beginning—and at every step of the way. The gifts we bear the infant Christ are the talents with which we have been blessed and which we must use for the glory of God. The Magi remind us that the life of faith is not based on static principles, but an adventure of great proportions that begins again with each new day. *Their* journey is *our* journey. When we ponder the Magi, we secretly ponder our own walk in faith. When we see them before the Christ child, bearing their gifts we wonder at what stage we ourselves are on in our journey and how long it will be before we reach our final destination.

7. *Proclamation, Adoration, and Work.* The angels and shepherds in the icon remind us of the importance of adoring God, proclaiming the message he has given us, and finding him in all things, especially in our work. The angels are representatives of the heavenly world. As messengers of the Lord, they remind

us that we too are called to share the Good News of Jesus' birth with those around us. The adoration of their newborn king directs us to do the same. The shepherds, by way of contrast, represent the simple and unsophisticated laborers of the world. They hear the Good News while they are tending their sheep in the fields and, like the angels, hasten to Jesus' side to adore him and to proclaim his name. The angels and shepherds remind us that "the heavens and the earth shall proclaim the glory of the Lord's name." In the light of these symbols, we need to ask ourselves: Where and when do we adore the Lord? How do we share him with others? Do we look for him in all things, even in our work? Like the angels and shepherds, we, too, are only peripheral characters in God's providential plan of salvation. Like them, we must do all we can to draw attention to the birth of the infant in the world and in our hearts.

8. *Sacramental Re-Birth.* When we ponder the sacramental action taking place around the icon's baptismal font, we are reminded of the role the Church plays in the ongoing transformation of the world. Baptism in its various forms (by water, by fire, and by desire) initiates new life in us. Through it, we are incorporated into the life, death, and resurrection of Jesus. In doing so, we become members of his body. For this reason, the birth of Jesus—that moment when his body first took physical, historical shape—has special significance for the believer.

35

Through baptism, Christ is born within our hearts and enters our world anew. Through its cleansing, life-giving action, the New Law, the Gospel message of love, is engraved in our hearts. The icon seeks to give us a deeper appreciation of the Church, its sacraments, and the spiritual family into which we are born. Jesus is the head of that family; Mary, its mother. We see ourselves in the child about to be baptized. We also recognize Christ and his Church. The icon asks us to reflect on our baptism and to ask ourselves if we have remained faithful to promises made there. It implores us to renew our commitment to live and die for Christ. It also bids us to examine our relationship to the body of Christ, the Church, and to make efforts to ease whatever tensions we may uncover.

CONCLUSION

Christmas is a season for all of us to enter more deeply into the mystery of the incarnation. As we have just seen, one way of doing that is for us to try to enter into its deep spiritual message. The Christian churches—both East and West—have discovered proven means for doing so. Although they use different mediums and emphasize diverse theological motifs, the nativity scene of the West and the icon of the nativity from the East spark our imagination and help us to enter into the dramatic, life-giving narrative of Christ's birth.

The human heart is the starting point for the new

creation initiated by the Christ event. It is there where the drama of the nativity has taken root and, to this very day, continues to grow. It is there where each of us has the opportunity to become once more "like a little child" who looks with longing hope, smiling joy, and eager expectation for the coming of God's reign.

Spiritual Exercise

If possible, find a nativity icon and spend some time before it. Observe the various symbols displayed on it and ponder their meaning. See if any new meanings reveal themselves to you as you reflect on the symbols of the cave, the manger, the swaddling clothes, the ox and ass, Mary and Joseph, the Magi, the shepherds and angels, and the baptismal font. Try not to rush. Let the symbols of the icon reveal themselves to you. After you have spent some time pondering the meaning of the icon, then spend some time before it in prayer. Do this by simply staring into the icon. Gaze upon it and let it gaze upon you. Open your heart to the mystery revealed there. Step through the window of your soul and speak to God in the silence of your heart. Spend some time before the icon. Allow yourself to be nurtured by its quiet, sacramental gaze. If for some reason you are unable to find a nativity icon, go to the nativity scene in your home and rearrange it in a way that best describes the spiritual state of your soul. One by one, identify the various characters in the display and try to enter into their thoughts. What are they thinking? What are they saying and to whom? Is anyone quiet? What else is on their minds?

Are they hiding anything from him? Do they have any doubts or difficulties? Which of these characters do you identify with most? Which would you most like to emulate? Why do you feel this way? If for some reason, you do not have access to a nativity scene, gather some drawing materials and sketch your own. Use the same set of questions to guide your reflection.

Prayer

Lord, during this season of Christmas joy, I ask you to help me to celebrate the mystery of your incarnation in the daily circumstances of my life. You who became human so that humanity might become divine want me to be a part of your new creation. Help me, Lord, to cooperate with your grace. Help me to ponder the symbols of this holy season so that they may speak to me of your love and reveal to me the great lengths you have gone to for my salvation. Help me to open my heart to you in prayer and to hold nothing back from you. As I celebrate this season, Lord, fill me with joy and help me to get in touch with the excitement and anticipation that characterized my childhood. Help me to see your presence in others. Enable me to enter their worlds, give myself to them, and become nourishment for them—as you did for me. Be close to me, Lord. Teach me how to love. Help me to love you more.

CHAPTER THREE

FAITH IN EVERYDAY LIFE: THE SEASON OF ORDINARY TIME

I saw Eternity the other night,
Like a great ring of pure and endless light,
All calm, as it was bright;
And round beneath it Time in hours, days, years,
Driven by the spheres
Like a vast shadow moved; in which the world
all her train were hurled.

HENRY VAUGHAN,
"THE WORLD"[1]

The color of Ordinary Time is green, a primary hue and universal symbol of Life. This season focuses on the day-to-day realities of the walk of faith. It relishes the regular course of daily living, the normal flow of circumstances. The Church gives two extended periods to the observance of Ordinary Time. The first comes between the end of the Christmas season and the

39

beginning of Lent; the second, between the end of the Easter season and the beginning of the new liturgical year. In this chapter, we will look at the first of these "more than ordinary" times of the year.

ORDINARY TIME: MEANINGS AND MISCONCEPTIONS

To begin with, we must overcome some of our common misconceptions of the season of Ordinary Time. If we are honest, most of us would probably admit that we give little thought to the important role that this season plays in our life of faith. We tend to look upon Advent, Christmas, Lent, and Easter as those seasons that shape our spiritual lives and move us to embrace the mystery of the Christ event with more fervor and devotion. The season of Ordinary Time, by way of contrast, is looked upon as little more than filler. It constitutes "everything else," those nondescript times that bring us from one important season to the next. Because Ordinary Time does not elicit from us the same depth of response as the other seasons of the liturgical year generally do, we tend to think of it as a secondary and, in some cases, even an inferior season. Ordinary Time may represent for us the dull, lackluster state of our everyday lives. It cannot come close to what the other seasons have to offer.

Part of the reason for this thinking has to do with the various nuances of the term "ordinary." It can mean anything from "superior" (in the sense of "proven and true") to "average" (in the sense of "customary and routine") to "inferior" (in the sense of "poor and common-place"). For some reason, when we hear the expression "Ordinary Time," most of us tend to think of the second and third definitions and give little thought to the first. In the context of the liturgical year, however, Ordinary Time closely linked with "*ordo*," the Latin word for "order." In this context, the season of Ordinary Time is closely linked to our daily "order" or "discipline" of life. Although its rituals are routine, there is nothing "average," "mediocre," or "inferior" about Ordinary Time. On the contrary, the season prescribes a daily regimen of Word and sacrament that enables the believing community to become better followers of Jesus Christ. In this sense, the first meaning of "ordinary" (as "proven" or "true") comes closer to naming the relevance of this season for our lives; that is, it tries to offer the best possible means for the believing community to walk the way of holiness.

The placement of Ordinary Time in the liturgical calendar reveals its two specific roles in the overall movement of the seasons. That movement of the liturgical year seeks to embrace all of Jesus' life and continues on in the life of his body, the Church. When seen in this light, the first part of Ordinary Time (the part between the seasons of Christmas and Lent) corresponds to the events of Jesus' public ministry and focuses on Jesus' preaching and healing. Because it begins where the Christmas season ends, however, this first part of Ordinary Time also includes (at least implicitly) all that is contained in Christ's so-called hidden life at Nazareth.

In contrast, the second period of Ordinary Time (the part between Easter season and the beginning of the new liturgical year) focuses on the significance of the Christ event for the life of the Church. During this time, the Spirit of Christ vivifies the people of God and seeks to extend the redemptive action of Christ to all times, all places, and all people.

FIRST PERIOD OF ORDINARY TIME

The first period of Ordinary Time provides us with a unique opportunity to examine our call to discipleship in the light of Jesus' public ministry. A helpful way of doing this—one that fits well with the movement of Ordinary Time away from the Christmas season and toward the beginning of Lent—is to examine the three movements of time as we perceive them in our lives: that is, as past, present, and future.

LOOKING BACK

Since the first part of Ordinary Time comes immediately after the Christmas season, it reminds us that much of our adult life—including our attitudes, choices, and relationships—have been at least partially shaped by our earlier life experiences, especially those of our infancy and early childhood. This season invites us to explore the kinds of experiences in Jesus' "hidden life" that helped to shape the man he was to become. It was during the first thirty years of his life that Jesus went through the normal stages of childhood, adolescence, and young adulthood. It was also during this time that he must have honed the skills of observation and storytelling that made him an effective preacher of the reign of God. This first period of Ordinary Time ignites our curiosity about the hidden, unknown life of Jesus. During these early weeks of Ordinary Time, we are reminded of the child, the young boy, the adolescent, and the young adult behind the fully grown man. Jesus' early experiences contributed greatly to his capacity to execute his prophetic mission to his people. For this reason, the Lord's hidden life at Nazareth is intimately connected to his public ministry.

During this time, we are also called to ponder our response to God's calling in the light of our earlier years. We need to look at our lives and ask ourselves just what it was in our past that led us to make the choices that have brought us to where we are today. A number of questions arise. What, for example, are your earliest recollections? Were they positive or negative? Did you feel loved as a child? neglected? abused? What concrete experiences can you provide to back up these feelings? Who had the greatest influence on your life? Who were your heroes and role models? What kind of friends did you hang out with? How did you respond to peer pressure? Are you proud or ashamed of the way you reacted? What attitudes were embedded in your psyche during your earliest years? Do you think there are any that you are not fully aware of? How could you get in touch with these "buried" attitudes? Are there any memories that continually come back to you? Do you feel you have been injured in any way during your early years of life?

Have the injuries healed, or do you still feel wounded? Have you grown stronger or weaker as a result? How did these injuries influence your relationship with others? How did they influence your relationship with God? Have you talked to God about it? What influences have your early life experiences had on your present situation? How did they affect the choices you made concerning the direction your life has taken? These are the kinds of questions that come to mind when we look back over our lives and try to uncover the influences that have brought us to our present situation.

Looking Around

As our reflections on this period of Ordinary Time deepen, our focus turns to the actual events of Jesus' public ministry. As we read the accounts of his Galilean ministry, we encounter a man of firm purpose who spoke from the heart out of a deep sense of compassion for the people. He used simple parables and metaphors to convey his message of God's love for his hearers. He charismatically attracted a number of loyal followers who accompanied him as he made his way across the countryside preaching the Good News and healing those who came to him with their physical, mental, and spiritual ills. Jesus' reputation as a miracle worker followed him wherever he went. He shared with others his deep love for the Father and taught them how to pray. He invited his listeners to put the interests of others before their own and chastised those who burdened others with man-made rules that got in the way of their relationship with the Father. Jesus aroused in others either deep loyalty, love, and devotion or the complete opposite. Jesus told people not what they wanted to hear, but what they needed to hear. His honesty and candor brought about the conversion of many lives. It also made him suspect by those who felt threatened by the changes that his words might bring. Throughout his public ministry, Jesus gave of himself so that others might find themselves. He shared his vision of the kingdom freely and openly with anyone who was willing to listen. His words came from the depths of his heart and were geared entirely toward revealing to others the deep bond of love that he shared with the Father.

The public ministry of Jesus gradually turns our thoughts toward the witness that we ourselves give to God in our daily affairs. Just as Jesus' hidden life at Nazareth eventually blossomed in a fruitful public witness of the Father's love for the world, in one way or another, so must ours. A number of questions arise as we look at our lives and try to see the various ways in which we give witness to the presence of God within us and in our midst.

Where, for example, do your true spiritual convictions lie? What do you feel strongly about? What are you willing to suffer or perhaps even die for? Jesus' public ministry was permeated by a strong sense of purpose and conviction. His words and actions reflected this deep commitment to his mission. In our own lives, we need to do likewise. Do you share your convictions with others or do you keep them from others by locking them up inside your heart and preventing them from seeing the light of day? More importantly, have you made an honest attempt to sift through your priorities in order to discover the direction your life should take? Do you bring your concerns to God in prayer? Do you open up your life to God and reveal every dimension of your being to him—the physical, emotional, mental, spiritual, and social? Do you share your belief and insights into God with others? Do you believe that the Father loves you just as he loved Jesus? Do you share that love with others? These and similar questions come to the fore when we ponder Jesus' public ministry in the context of our own lives. Answering these questions requires courage. It is easy for us to entertain strong convictions in the inner sanctum of our hearts. It is quite another, however, to allow them to shape our agenda for action and to present them openly in a public forum. Jesus had the courage to do so. Are we are willing and able to follow his example?

LOOKING FORWARD

This first period of Ordinary Time gradually leads us to the beginning of the Lenten season. As this change of season approaches, our gaze gradually turns from Jesus' Galilean ministry to the events that led him to turn his face toward Jerusalem. As his ministry progresses, Jesus senses that the Father is asking him to make the ultimate sacrifice. Perhaps this knowledge came to him when he was driven into the desert after his baptism to undergo the temptations that would seek to divert him away from his ministry and message. Perhaps it was the untimely death of John the Baptist that drove him once again to a deserted place where he could struggle yet again with the purpose of his mission and his discernment of the Father's will. Perhaps it was his perception that he had pushed the authorities too far and that the Romans and Jewish authorities would not tolerate him very much longer. Whenever it occurred, Jesus clearly senses imminent danger and even begins to predict his approaching passion and death. This looming danger, however, does not make him waver in his mission to preach the coming of the reign of God. On the contrary, it makes him even more determined to see his mission to its end. This first period of Ordinary Time invites us to participate in the great sense of urgency that grows to heightened proportions during the last days of his public ministry. It asks us to travel with Jesus as he makes his way by foot across the Galilean countryside this one last time until he makes his way up to Jerusalem to meet his destiny and to carry out the will of his Father.

Jesus' journey to Jerusalem challenges us to ponder our own destination in life. A sense of our own mortality should make us urgently consider how to live the life God has given us to the full. It should sharpen our sight about the things in life that really matter and deepen our insight into the meaning of our journey. Sooner or later, each of us must join Jesus in his journey to Jerusalem. When that time comes we can renew our commitment to follow him as a faithful disciple or we can look for a way to escape our fate. Once again, a number of questions arise. Are you anxious about dying? Are you looking for a way to ignore or escape it? Is God's love all that really matters to you? What are you still holding on to in life? What are you afraid to let go of? Jesus understood that the best way to celebrate life was to turn it over to his Father. Can you say the same for yourself? Have you placed your life in God's hands? Do you trust God with your life? Do you believe that he will not allow any harm to come to you? Only by letting go of life in this way will you come to discover its true worth. This period of Ordinary Time bids us to seize the moment and to live life with the urgency that sent Jesus to Jerusalem to complete his execution of the Father's will. It asks us to consider our own mission in life—whatever it may be—and to dedicate ourselves to it with strength and determination. As we journey through these weeks of Ordinary Time, we try to live more in the present moment. We see that our lives are intertwined with the life of Jesus, and we gradually come to understand that his final journey to Jerusalem is very much our own.

THE CALL TO SIMPLE LIVING

Looking back. Looking around. Looking forward. These three dimensions of this period of Ordinary Time represent a call to simple living. One way to understand this focus on simple living is to view it against the backdrop of the other seasons that makeup the Church's liturgical year. In general, there are three types of seasons: (1) those involving preparation (Advent and Lent); (2) those involving celebration (Christmas and Easter); and (3) those involving the simple routines of daily living (the two periods of Ordinary Time). This classification provides us with the general pulse of the seasons as they move in succession from one to the next. This rhythm of preparation, celebration, and daily living occurs twice during the liturgical year (that is, Advent/Christmas/Ordinary Time and Lent/Easter/Ordinary Time). We have already seen that the first period of Ordinary Time takes into consideration past, present, and future as it moves the believing community away from the Christmas season and brings it to the opening day of Lent. In doing so, it plays two important roles for the faithful. In the first place, Ordinary Time completes the Advent/Christmas cycle by emphasizing the importance of living the Christian message in the normal affairs of life. It reminds us that our faith comes to full fruition only when it permeates every aspect of our lives. It encourages us to allow all the preparations and joyous celebration of the previous months to change our perspective and to influence our lives. It tells us that we must not only prepare for Christmas but also allow its message of God's love for the world to have an effect on the way we live our lives. The first period of Ordinary Time brings the Advent/Christmas cycle to a natural close. It represents the afterglow of the great season of warmth and good cheer. It reminds us, moreover, that the Word became flesh some two thousand years ago and wishes to do so again in our lives this very day, that this Good News needs to become a part of the warp and woof of our everyday lives. The first period of Ordinary Time takes the focus away from all the preparation and celebration that have gone into the Christmas season and places the emphasis on living the message of Christ in the normal circumstances of our lives. It is a predictable season, but it is by no means inferior to those that have preceded it. On the contrary, one can easily make the argument that only after the seasons of Advent and Christmas have passed can we measure the extent to which we have truly taken their message to heart. For this reason, it is an indispensable element of our ongoing walk with the Lord.

In the second place, the first period of Ordinary Time performs an important transitional function by filling the gap between Christmas and Lent. In doing so, it gives us the necessary distance to appreciate the significance of what has just taken place and what is about to occur. This status as an "in-between season" matches its character perfectly. Our daily lives are full of similar "in-between" moments. Most of us tend to measure our lives in terms of the extraordinary things that happen to us (for example, a wedding, the birth of a child, a long-awaited promotion). Most of life, however, consists of nothing but a series of long, in-between periods of time that we fill with the simple, tedious (and often monotonous) tasks of daily life. The season of Ordinary Time reminds us that Jesus, the Lord of History, wishes to be present to us even at moments such as these. It encourages us to recognize all of life as a gift and to live each moment to the fullest. Jesus, it is said, entered our world and carried out the Father's plan of redemption "...in the fullness time" (Eph 1:10). He did so, however, in very humble and ordinary circumstances. Ordinary Time reminds us that all of time (even the in-between moments) has been redeemed by Christ and will in someway participate in the new creation that he initiated at his birth. It also reminds us that we are all presently living in an in-between time, the one that bridges Christ's first and second comings. When seen in this light, all of us are presently living during an extended season of Ordinary Time that already has spanned a number of centuries and may very well fill up a great many more. Ordinary Time reminds us that the monotony of life can itself be redeemed. It encourages us to live in the present moment and to find in its pregnant silences a faint but clearly recognizable trace of the eternal.

CONCLUSION

The season of Ordinary Time is divided into two periods and makes up the greater part of the Church's liturgical year—a full thirty-four weeks. The sheer size of the season speaks to us of its importance. Unfortunately, most of us are unimpressed by this and tend to take the season for granted. We fail to see that it provides the backdrop against which the other liturgical seasons arise, take shape, and are ultimately measured. We find it difficult to get excited over Ordinary Time and often look upon it as a dull, humdrum season that reflects the dreary monotony of everyday life. As a result, we overlook its deep, resilient nature.

Ordinary Time is many things, but it is far from ordinary. Without it, we would lose sight of the continuity and dynamic movement of the liturgical seasons. Without it, we would fail to appreciate the truly remarkable things that happen in life. Ordinary Time reminds us that Christ came to redeem all of creation, including space and time. It tells us that the latter is like slowly fermenting grapes that will one day receive a different texture and taste. It encourages us to look at the ordinary events of our lives with the wonder of a child and the eyes of faith: "I assure you, unless you change and become like little children, you will not enter the kingdom of God" (Mt 18:3). Have you ever noticed how a little child can find cause for wonder in even the simplest and most routine actions of daily life?

The first period of Ordinary Time rounds out the cycle of preparation, celebration, and daily living that is characteristic of the Christmas season. It also helps the believing community to settle down after a festive holiday season and to ready itself for the approaching Lenten season. It does so by enabling us to look back at what has taken place, to appreciate what is going on around us, and to anticipate what is yet to come. Ordinary Time is both our time and the Lord's time. It invites us not only to find God's presence in the most routine tasks of daily life but also to perform those tasks with a spirit of praise and thanksgiving. Ordinary Time offers us the opportunity to make sacred the everyday events of our lives. It brings us to the threshold of the holy and makes every day a holy day—and that makes all the difference.

Spiritual Exercise

Get a timer or an alarm clock and set it for five minutes. Then close your eyes and try to count the movement of the seconds. When you think you have reached the five-minute limit, open your eyes and see how close you came to the mark. Did the timer go off before or after your count? Were you rushing the count or slowing it down? Do you think you would improve if you tried it again? After this brief exercise, try to write down as many positive points about chronological time that you can think of. When you have finished, try listing all its negative aspects. When you have finished, look at the lists and see which one is longer. Do you enjoy living in chronological time? What impact does this measured experience of time have on the season of Ordinary Time? Next, go somewhere where you like to go to get away for a while: a spot under a tree, a nice easy chair, a place in a chapel. Close your eyes and try to relax. In a quiet whisper or silently in your heart, start saying the words of the Jesus Prayer: "Lord Jesus, have mercy on me. Lord Jesus, have mercy on me." Try not to think of anything. Simply say the words and let your mind wander. Try not to keep track of time. Just let yourself go. Allow the words to penetrate your breathing. Allow them to touch the beating of your heart. Remain perfectly still and lose yourself in the present moment. Do nothing else but pray the Jesus Prayer and live in the present moment. Do not even think of stopping. When you open your eyes, write down what your experience of the present moment was like. List its positive and negative aspects. What impact does this experience of sacred time have on the season of Ordinary Time? As you look back over your life, which experience of time has most influenced your life? Which do you prefer? What steps can you take to experience more of it? Are *Chronos* (chronological time) and *Kairos* (sacred time) contradictory or complementary? Could they in any way be both? Can one be transformed into the other? If so, how?

Prayer

Lord, during this initial period of Ordinary Time, help me to live the call to simple living. Let me use this time between Christmas and Lent to ponder the meaning of my life here on earth. Enable me to look to your hidden life in Nazareth and to your public ministry in Galilee as a point of reference for the way I should walk. Help me, Lord, to remember my past with gratitude, to live my present life with care, and to look to the future with ardent hope. Help me to bring a patient, joyful, and caring heart to each moment. Help me to appreciate the circumstances of my life and to let you be a part of them. Help me to look for you in the people I meet and in my normal, everyday activities. Help me to offer up even my boring and monotonous moments to you, Lord. Enable me to look for the extraordinary in the ordinary. Help me to live in the present moment. Let everything I do in my life be done for you. I love you, Lord. Help me to love you more.

CHAPTER FOUR

CHANGING OUR HEARTS: THE SEASON OF THE LENTEN CROSS

Nothing is so beautiful as Spring—
When weeds, in wheels, shoot long and
lovely and lush;
Thrush's eggs look like little low heavens,
and thrush
Through the echoing timber does
so rinse and wring
The ear, it strikes like lightnings
to hear him sing;
The glassy peartree leaves and blooms,
they brush
The descending blue; that blue is all in a rush
With richness; the racing lambs too have fair
their fling.

GERARD MANLEY HOPKINS,
"SPRING"[1]

The word "Lent" comes from an Anglo-Saxon word for "spring." It is a season for preparing our hearts for the Good News of Christ's Easter Pasch. We do so by adopting a balanced regimen of prayer and penance. Lent is a season of change, a period of forty days and forty nights for us to take stock of our lives and to ready ourselves for Christ's suffering, death, and resurrection. According to Saint Ambrose of Milan (c. 339–97), it is "the acceptable time...the day of our salvation," a season when all of us "...must be more earnest in prayer and in fasting, in almsgiving and in watching."[2]

LESS THAN SKIN-DEEP

If I am to be honest, I must admit that Lent is not a season I have regularly looked forward to. More often than not, it has been a period of time simply to get through, a trial to be endured, a burden to be patiently borne.

For much of my early life, *the* most important part of Lent was getting the ashen cross signed on my forehead during Ash Wednesday services. I took part in this yearly ritual not necessarily because I wanted to be reminded that I was dust and one day would return to dust, but because I simply wanted to parade around the neighborhood showing others how pious and holy I was. I wasn't exactly what today we would call an "Ash Wednesday Catholic." I went to weekly Mass and did most of the things expected of me by my faith—at least externally. However, my attitude toward the season was not substantially different from those whose practice of the faith amounted to nothing more than an annual trip to their parish church to get ashes.

In the predominantly Catholic environment of my youth, it was easy to pamper myself with this external expression of the faith. When I moved away to college, however, I found myself in a sizable minority and started to feel embarrassed by the visible mark of the faith on my forehead. To ease my discomfort, I eventually found myself doing one of three things: (1) washing the ashes off as soon as possible; (2) convincing myself that I was too busy to go for them; or (3) conveniently forgetting that it was Ash Wednesday. It took me a long time to realize that my faith was very much less than skin-deep. It took me even longer to understand that the external symbols of the faith need to enter our hearts and penetrate our minds if they are to bring concrete results in our lives.

PRAYER IN THE GARDEN

Lent is not a time for us to display our religion so that others can see it. Jesus himself warned against such tactics (Mt 6:16–18). Nor is it a time to conceal it out of convenience or to reject it out of fear of what others might think of us (Lk 11:33). Those who do so will themselves be dealt with in a similar manner (Jn 12:48). Lent is a time for us to come face to face with our disordered love of self. We do so by allowing the deep wounds of self-centeredness to surface within our hearts so that we can examine them and present them to God for cleansing and healing. The purifying power of Lent comes through the action of God's grace that inspires us to lead a life of prayer and penitence. Lent readies us for our encounter with the Risen Lord on Easter morning.

Lent is a season of spring for the soul. It is a time when bad habits are weeded out and the seeds of good ones planted, watered, and allowed to grow. Lent is very much about taking off the old self and putting on the new (Col 3:9–10). It encourages us to put the life of sin behind us and to embrace the love of God and the life of virtue. Such a life, however, has a social dimension to it. Thus, our practice of Lent is not meant to be a private affair but a community effort. As the people of God, we need to celebrate together, serve together, and journey together. It is also important for us to examine all of our relationships—personal, family, communal, societal—to find the dysfunctional ways of relating that have crept into our lives so that we can lay them before the Lord. We must discover new ways of relating to one another based on dignity and respect, dialogue and understanding, mercy and forgiveness. Lent reminds us that it is never too late to turn away from our self-centered grievances and walk the way of conversion. Such penitent conversion gives the Holy Spirit a foothold in our lives. Through the Spirit's various gifts (Isa 11:2–3) and fruits (Gal 5:22–23), it builds up the body of Christ on earth and furthers Christ's mission to spread the Good News of God's love to the furthest corners of the earth.

Another way of saying this is that our Lenten practice should make us better disciples. We become better disciples only by sitting at the feet of Our Lord, asking him to teach us, listening to what he has to say to us, and then carrying it out. We accomplish this by praying to God with open hearts, immersing ourselves in the Scriptures, participating in the sacraments, and allowing the symbols and practices of Lent to speak to us. In this way, the season of Lent becomes very much like a time of retreat where the Church's members (and those soon to become members) have an opportunity to enter more deeply into their baptismal promises. This time enables us to look at what really matters in life. With it, we come to know Christ more intimately and see how much his passion, death, and resurrection mean to us. Without it, discipleship gradually moves to the periphery of our consciousness, and our identity as Christians becomes diluted and compromised.

To be a Christian means to be "a follower of the Way." The way of the Lord Jesus is that of selfless surrender to the will of the Father. "*Abba* (O Father), you have the power to do all things. Take this cup away from me. But let it be as you would have it, not as I" (Mk 14:36). These words of Jesus in the Garden of Gethsemane come from his final moments of solitude before his horrible suffering and death by crucifixion. The chief elements of this episode are Jesus' intense prayer to the Father and his resigned acceptance of his approaching death as a part of God's plan for the world. We should celebrate Lent in a similar way. We should look to it as our time of silent retreat when we open ourselves up to

God in prayer, deepen our relationship with the Father, and ask for the grace to conform our will to his.

THE ASHEN CROSS

The ashen cross that opens the season of Lent is a symbol of penitence. In biblical times, sackcloth and ashes were the external manifestations of repentance. The mark of the ashen cross continues this tradition into the present. Made from the ashes of the leftover palms from the Passion Sunday celebration of the previous year, the sign evokes the memory of Christ's triumphant entry into Jerusalem and the tragic events that were soon to follow. Now, when the sign is given, the priest or deacon has the option of saying the traditional, "Remember you are dust…" phrase or another response that also focuses on the spirit of the Lenten season: "Turn away from sin and be faithful to the Gospel." Each saying has a special significance for the time ahead.

The first response recalls God's words to Adam in the Garden immediately after the Fall (Gen 3:19) and reminds us that death looms on the horizon of every human being. Many of us are afraid to face this cold, harsh fact and will go to great lengths to put the thought of death out of our minds. Western culture goes out of its way to divert our attention away from thoughts of death. All this, however, has little effect. It is impossible to deceive death or to postpone the inevitable. Sooner or later, our final hour approaches. It may give us fair warning or come without us knowing it, as Jesus said of the Son of Man, "like a thief in the night." The ashen cross reminds us from where we have come and to where we must one day return. Just as the ashes themselves will gradually fade away with the passage of time, so will we. The question for each of us is whether we have prepared ourselves for what lies ahead.

The second response puts us in close contact with Jesus' original Gospel message (Mk 1:15). In doing so, it brings to the fore the importance in our lives of our personal encounter with Christ. All the penitential practices in the world would be of little avail if they did not help us to come to know Christ in a deeper, more intimate way. So often in the past, Christians (and Catholics especially) have used external signs of devotion as a way of deepening their relationship with God. While such practices are helpful, they can just as easily be mistaken for the relationship itself. When this occurs, we make an idol of the very things designed to foster our relationship with God. The practice of religion then takes the place of God's action in our lives, and we gradually become shallow and superficial. Our "spirituality" becomes more and more wrapped up in externals and, if we are not careful, will closely resemble the false kind of religiosity for which the scribes and the Pharisees were accused (for example, Mt 23:1–39). The words of this response remind us that externals are important only to the extent that they facilitate inner conversion and a change of heart. The repentance called for in this saying is precisely that which enables us to look inside our hearts and ask God's pardon for the sins we have committed.

Once again, we come face to face with our pride and self-centeredness. We cannot change if we refuse to ask God for help. So many of us, however, either believe we have no need to change or that we can do it all by ourselves.

The ashen cross and the words that accompany it are concrete reminders that the season of Lent calls for an interior conversion that will bring corresponding changes to the way we live our lives. In this way, our external actions of faith become deeply felt expressions of heart, manifestations of what we believe deep down and what, like the Lord Jesus himself, are willing to die for.

The Way of Conversion

The ashen cross on our foreheads is an outward sign of our deep desire for inner conversion. This interior change of heart comes about by being "…more earnest in prayer and in fasting, in almsgiving and in watching." An easy way to remember these forms of Lenten penance is to think of each one in the context of the simple prayer known as the "sign of the cross." A correlation of these various activities with the appropriate part of the sign of the cross would look like this.

1. *In Prayer.* We begin the sign of the cross by bringing the tips of our right hand to our forehead and saying, "In the name of the Father." This first movement of the sign of the cross corresponds to the very

activity of prayer itself. By touching our foreheads we call attention to the rational side of our natures. This side embraces both our intellects and our wills, two facets of our human makeup that are integral to the life of prayer. To lift our hearts and minds to God is another way of saying that we must orient our intellect and will to the Lord. In doing so, we offer the most noble dimensions of who we are to God. As a result, a process is initiated whereby the other elements of our nature follow suit. The life of prayer then becomes an integral part of our lives. Although there are many forms of prayer, all of them in some way involve raising our hearts and minds to God. The season of Lent is a time when we are asked to be especially earnest in our life of prayer. This seriousness of intent applies to individuals and to their communities. During this time, we need to take a good look at the way we pray—both privately and in groups—and ask ourselves if we are truly acting with our whole heart, mind, soul, and strength. Lent offers us a good opportunity to see to what extent the various dimensions of our human makeup—the physical, intellectual, emotional, spiritual, and social—enter into our prayer.

2. *In Fasting.* We continue the sign of the cross by extending the tips of our right hand down to our stomachs and saying, "...and of the Son." Touching this part of our anatomy during our prayer highlights the physical, animal aspect of our human nature.

Our gut is often considered the seat of the emotions—
that part of us which controls our urges for food
and drink, that part of us which controls our urges
for sexual pleasure and arousal, and that part which
controls our ability to display anger and sadness.
The downward movement of our hand during the
sign of the cross together with the reference to God's
Son is a clear indication of the mystery of the incarnation. "The Word became flesh and made his dwell-
ing among us" (Jn 1:14). The appropriateness of this
correlation between the downward movement of our
hands to our gut and the Second Person of the Trinity is plainly obvious. The Word of God assumed
our human nature. In doing so, he took on not only
our capacity to think and choose but also to feel
emotions and to experience the world through the
bodily senses. According to Scripture, Jesus "...was
tempted in every way that we are, yet never sinned"
(Heb 4:15). His virtuous life extended to his passions and animal nature and was exhibited most
clearly through his courage and temperate living.
Those of us who seek to be his disciples must try to
do likewise. We can imitate Jesus in this way only
by calling on his name and asking him for help. When
seen in this light, the word "fasting" and its associated term "abstinence" take on new meaning. They
refer not merely to the intake of food and drink (one
full meal a day with regard to fasting; refraining from
particular foods with regards to abstinence), but to
the wide range of sensations that affect the seat of

our emotions. The season of Lent provides us with an opportunity to examine the ways in which we have been excessive in our pursuit of pleasure and in our display of spirited emotion. During this time, it is important for us to identify ways to temper our bodily and emotional lives so that they will give honor and glory to God. All true fasting is a way of emptying ourselves for the Lord. It is an action done for God and with the help of God. In its intent, it is always closely associated with the act of prayer.

3. *In Almsgiving.* We continue the sign of the cross by extending the tips of our right hand over to our left shoulder and saying "...and of the Holy." This part of the sign of the cross moves away from the vertical and begins the important horizontal movement of the prayer, that part which is normally associated with love of neighbor. It is appropriate, therefore, that the penitential action associated with this aspect of the prayer would be "almsgiving." Our prayer to God manifests itself in our love of others. Extending charity to those in need has strong biblical roots (for example, Mt 6:1–4 ; Rom 12:3–8). It is an expression of concern for our fellow human beings, giving an indication of their inherent human dignity. As his followers, we understand that we can express love for God in and through our love for our neighbors. As the parable of the Good Samaritan attests (Lk 10:25–37), our neighbor is not just the person who lives next door, but *anyone* who

needs our help. When we give to others, we should
give beyond our capacity, not merely from our ex-
cess wealth (Mk 12:41–44). We should do so not
only to our friends and family but also to strangers
in need, the poor and needy—and even to our en-
emies (Mt 5:43–48). When we give of ourselves in
this way, we should be sincere in what we do, re-
spectful of those we give to, generous with our hos-
pitality, and extending the same attitude toward all
(Rom 12:9–21). Because God loves us, we should
seek to extend his love to others. It is through actions such as these that God's presence is made manifest on the earth. During the season of Lent, we seek
to make that presence even more visible. Giving to
others is an external sign of our internal conversion
of heart. We should be conscious, moreover, not only
of *how much* and *to whom* we give but also *how* we
give to others. We must not give sadly or grudg-
ingly, but with great joy: "God loves a cheerful giver"
(2 Cor 9:7; Rom 12:8).

4. *In Watching.* We complete the sign of the cross by
extending the tips of our right hand in one sweeping
motion across our chest to our right shoulder and
saying the word "Spirit." This action corresponds
to our fourth Lenten practice of "watchfulness in
the Spirit." Vigilance is a necessary part of the spiritual life. We do so in order to anticipate and avoid
whatever dangers might await us and to seize those
positive opportunities that come around and, if not

taken advantage of, can easily pass us by. We need to be watchful with respect to ourselves, others, and the Lord. As far as we are concerned, it is important for us to be on the lookout for those subtle ways in which we deceive ourselves. It is so easy for us to do harm to ourselves without even knowing it, in fact, even while thinking we are helping ourselves along. Lent is a time to take a good look at our lives and to identify any attitudes and behaviors having a negative effect on us. It is also a time to look out for new and creative ways of enhancing our spiritual growth. A lack of vigilance in our lives often results in a breakdown of our ability to defend ourselves against threats to our well being and to discover new venues for developing our deepest potential. The same holds true for our relations with others. We are social beings. So much of who we are and what we do is intimately linked to the kinds of friendships we form and the various communities to which we belong. If we are not vigilant in maintaining these relationships, they can easily become dysfunctional. As a result, they can do great harm. Lent is a time for examining the social dimension of our lives and to root out whatever harmful attitudes or ways of relating have entered into them. It is also a time for finding and implementing new ways of relating that will improve the quality of our lives in community. In this way, our friendships, families, and communities will reflect a bit more clearly the Gospel values that we embrace and wish to reflect to the larger world around us. Finally, our watchfulness must also extend to God. In this regard, we need to ask ourselves if we have allowed any false images of God to take hold of us and to influence our attitudes and behaviors. These idols must be recognized for what they are and struck down so that the one true God might reign in our hearts. Lent is a time for finding new ways of nurturing our relationship with the divine. Just as people become close friends by spending time with one another, so, too, can we deepen our relationship with God by looking out for ways of being present to him in the daily circumstances of our lives.

Prayer. Fasting. Almsgiving. Watchfulness. Saint Ambrose reminds us that we should perform these Lenten practices "with earnestness." This sacred season challenges us to get over our tepid practice of the faith and to open our hearts to the Lord with fervent love and devotion. The Scriptures tell us of the consequences for those who do otherwise: "I know your deeds; I know you are neither hot nor cold. How I wish you were one or the other—hot or cold! But because you are lukewarm, neither hot nor cold, I will spew you out of my mouth!" (Rev 3:15). Calculated indifference and simple lack of interest are among the greatest threats to the faith today. People believe and practice their faith with a minimalist mind-set. They go for the least common denominator and leave everything else open to personal preference. As a result, they pick and choose what to believe and what not to believe in much the same way that they would shop at a supermarket or select an entree from a menu at a restaurant.

Lent is a time for putting things back in perspective. It seeks to shake us out of our stupor so that we can recognize that our relationship with God is all-important. Prayer, fasting, almsgiving, and watchfulness are four ways through which we can move out of our indifference toward God and come to experience him with a deep desire and a burning heart. Themselves intimately related, these practices orient our hearts anew toward the Church's sacramental and devotional life and bring new meaning to the ashen cross which marks our foreheads at the outset of this great season. They also inject new life into a simple prayer that most of us have said over and over again without reflection.

CONCLUSION

Lent is a season of repentance. It offers us an opportunity to turn our lives around and be converted to the Lord. Heartfelt conversions of this type occur in a variety of ways and can begin at any time and in any place. One way that has withstood the test of time is to adopt a steady but gentle discipline of daily Lenten practice.

The ashen cross placed on our foreheads at the start of Lent is a vivid reminder of what Christ asks of his followers: "Whoever puts his hand to the plow but keeps looking back is unfit for the reign of God" (Lk 9:62). We who are dust bear the hope of eternal life only because of the feat accomplished by Christ when he faced his own humiliation on the cross. Jesus did not look back; neither should we. During Lent, we are called upon to come to a deeper understanding of our relationship to the suffering Christ. We are encouraged to explore the possibility that our own trials might be somehow intimately related to his. Our acts of Lenten penance symbolize our desire to conform our hearts and minds to God's. Only in this way can we deepen our encounter with the Lord and walk down the long and treacherous path of selfless love.

Lent is not an end in itself, but a period of preparation. During that time, everything we do should be done under the sign of the cross. Prayer, fasting, almsgiving, and watchfulness guard the ends of the vertical and horizontal crossbeams. Their point of intersection belongs to (and is borne by) the love in our hearts. The symbolism depicted here speaks for itself: conversion of heart is closely bound up with the crosses we shoulder and the paths we walk. Those who follow the Lord and who call themselves his disciples see conversion as an ongoing process that takes a lifetime to accomplish—sometimes more. As we journey through Lent, we prepare our hearts for the difficult road ahead of us in life and in death. In the course of forty days and nights, we have the opportunity to look again at the promises we made at baptism and choose either to renew them or to turn away from them. We renew them by embracing the Lenten cross with its fourfold regimen of prayer, fasting, almsgiving, and watchfulness; we turn away from them by ignoring them, by being indifferent to them, or by simply rejecting them outright.

Spiritual Exercise

Find a quiet place where you can be alone with God. Get in a comfortable yet prayerful position, one that you sustain for a few minutes. When you are ready, open your heart and mind to God with the sign of the cross. Perform this prayer very slowly. Say the words out loud or quietly to yourself: "In the name of the Father, and of the Son, and of the Holy Spirit. Amen." When you have finished, pause a moment and then start over. This time, be conscious of the parts of your body that you are touching as you say the prayer: your head, the seat of your rational powers; your stomach, the seat of your emotions; and your shoulders, the part of you which bears physical burdens and performs daily labor. When you have finished, pause a moment and say the prayer once more. When you touch your head and say the words, "In the name of the Father," ask the Lord to make your reason and your will completely centered on his love. When you touch your stomach and say the words, "...and of the Son," ask the Lord to heal your emotions so that you will be able to feel God's love and express it to others in appropriate ways. When you touch your shoulders and say the words, "...and of the Holy Spirit," ask the Lord to bless your body and to help you to rid yourself of any physical attachments that may be getting in the way of your relationship with him. When you have finished, pause a moment and say the prayer one last time. As you say the prayer, be conscious of the vertical and horizontal motion of your hands. When you touch your head, ask the Lord to help you to be a prayerful person. When you touch your stomach, ask the Lord to help you to be a temperate person. When you touch your left shoulder, ask the Lord to help you to be a generous person. When you touch your right shoulder, ask the Lord to help you to be a watchful person. When you say, "Amen," ask the Lord to help you to express your love for him in and through your love for others.

Prayer

Lord, during this season of the Lenten cross, help me to turn my life entirely over to you so that I might become a devoted disciple and follower of your way. Enable me to look beneath the external trappings of the season and to ponder its deep spiritual significance. Change me, Lord. Convert me, Lord. Guide me along the way of repentance. Show me my sins and give me the courage to confess them. Teach me how to pray, Lord. Help me to make sacrifices for you. Enable me to be generous with others. Help me to keep watch over my relationship with you and not allow anyone or anything to interfere with it. Reveal my weaknesses to me, Lord. Steer me clear of temptation. Help me to let go of the unnecessary attachments that have gotten in the way and have kept me from you. Help me to turn to you always, in good times as well as in bad. I love you, Lord. Help me to love you more.

CHAPTER FIVE

"HE IS RISEN!"
THE SEASON OF EASTER
PROCLAMATION

All night had shout of men and cry
Of woeful women filled His way;
Until that noon of sombre sky
On Friday, clamour and display
Smote Him; no solitude had He,
No silence, since Gethsemane.

Public was Death; but Power, but Might,
But Life again, but Victory,
Were hushed within the dead of night,
The shutter'd dark, the secrecy.
And all alone, alone, alone
He rose again behind the stone.

ALICE MEYNELL,
"EASTER NIGHT"[1]

For Christians, Jesus' resurrection from the dead is the central mystery of their faith and sets their religion apart from all others. When pressed, they will be able to offer very few details about this event. The empty tomb, the testimony of a few women, the conviction of the apostles and the early Christian community are nearly all they have to go on. Scholars have combed the Gospel accounts of Jesus' resurrection and concluded that, because they are primarily documents of faith, it is impossible to determine with historical accuracy precisely what occurred. Those inclined toward belief will focus on the faith of those who produced them and insist that something of substance must be behind their experience. Those inclined toward skepticism will emphasize the capacity human beings have to convince themselves of almost anything. For those who believe, however, the proclamation of Easter morning is precisely what is to be expected from an all-powerful and all-loving God. It is the resurrection event that maintains a continuity between our present bodily condition and our transformed state in the life to come.

METAPHORS OF RESURRECTION

Metaphors for the resurrection abound in nature. Seeds must be buried in the earth and die before they sprout victoriously in the spring and bear the fruits of harvest. Caterpillars weave cocoons around themselves and are gradually transformed into fluttering butterflies. Lizards, snakes, and other reptiles retreat into a low-metabolic, deathlike state during their months of hibernation only to awake in the spring from their long wintry sleep. We ourselves undergo numerous biological transformations from the moment of conception to the time of death. We enter the light of day from the darkened constraints of our mothers' wombs. We take in food and drink and gradually change it into our own flesh and blood. These are but a few of the ways in which the book of creation provides us with telling signs of the world to come.

Unfortunately, many of us have forgotten how to ponder the traces of the Divine in the world around us. We have adopted a viewpoint that thinks the earth's only purpose is to serve our bodily, material needs. We have lost touch with the material world and somehow feel as though we can do what we wish with it. This attitude manifests itself in a variety of ways. We litter, pollute, deforest, deplete, and deprive our environment of its rich resources. We put little, if anything, back. We alienate ourselves from the world and from our place in it. Because we fail to contemplate the simple, everyday signs and wonders that surround us, we sink more readily into loneliness and isolation and become easy prey for the disturbing voices of doubt and uncertainty. Instead of thinking that the material world will reveal the beyond to us, we look upon it as a hindrance, as something that keeps us back from finding and developing our deepest humanity. We consider it a burden to be overcome, a chain that ties us down.

We are an integral part of the world in which we live. Once we lose contact with it, we begin also to lose touch with ourselves, with others, and with God. Our failure to contemplate the world around us and to ponder the vestiges of the beyond imprinted in it by God cannot help but have a negative effect on our relationships. With such a desacralized view of the world, it does not take long before we begin treating other people in a manipulative and dehumanizing way. We forget how to acknowledge their deep inner goodness and begin to think that we can use them for our own purposes. To tap the rich resources within us, we need to rekindle in our hearts the desire to meditate on creation and to decipher its vast array of signs and symbols. If we did so with open and sincere hearts, we would be surprised that our discoveries are a great cause for celebration.

COMPETING NARRATIVES

One would think that, since the resurrection outshines all other notions of the afterlife, people would flock to Christianity in droves. The contrary, however, seems to be the case—at least in Western culture. As our fascination with oriental religions, new-age mysticism, and the occult attests, resurrection as a belief no longer attracts as large a genuinely convinced group of believers as it once did. That is not to say that the concept is rejected outright. It simply means that it is accepted halfheartedly and no longer shapes the way we live our lives. We have learned to go through the motions of the Church's collective belief, while reserving the right to entertain our own eclectic thoughts on the matter. We can recite the creed by rote, but, for many of us, the words have lost their ability to engender any deep religious conviction. The words fail to register, making little headway in the sea of uncertainties that cloud our minds.

In the past, Christians were so taken up with the mystery of the resurrection that the Church felt a need to set aside more and more days for celebrating the feast. In time, a single day for celebrating the paschal mystery gradually turned into a triduum (three days) and then into an entire octave (eight days). The present season of Easter, the fifty days from the Easter Vigil to the feast of Pentecost, has its roots in the Church's efforts to enable the faithful to reflect on as many aspects of Christ's paschal mystery as possible. Today, the Church retains the fifty-day season, but many of us have long forgotten its purpose. Instead of seeking relevance in the various facets of the Christ event, we allow other narratives—both sacred and secular—to fill our imaginations and shape our lives. Today, the Easter narrative must compete for our attention with secular narratives of enormous power. Which will capture our hearts is difficult to say.

One such narrative of particular power is that of "The American Dream." Most of us already know its particulars. From the moment we get up in the morning, we are bombarded by media messages about what we need to make our lives complete. The list gets larger with every generation: a bigger house, another car, an outdoor pool, expensive furniture, a country retreat, and so on. These messages have actually convinced us that the quality of our lives depends on the things we possess. As a result, we work long hours to make enough money so that we can buy the things that we are told we need to lead happy, productive lives. We work ourselves to the bone in order to live up to a very superficial standard of success. More often than not, we are too tired to enjoy them when we finally do find some free moments in our busy schedules. In the end, our quick-paced lives spin out of control, and our possessions end up taking possession of us.

For most of us, this dream of material success in the land of opportunity seems to be much more deeply rooted in our value system than the narrative of Jesus' passion, death, and resurrection. Both narratives touch extremely important sectors of our lives, and we have somehow convinced ourselves that they can co-exist in a relative state of peace. Such a judgment, however, could not be further from the truth. The underlying values of one narrative are deeply at odds with those of the other. Jesus' words to the rich young man to sell his possessions and give to the poor (Mt 19:21) may not have been intended for everyone, but the spirit that inspired those words is antagonistic to America's idea of material success.

KEY ELEMENTS OF THE EASTER PROCLAMATION

The only way we can transcend the confusion brought about by these competing narratives is to step back and look at them in detail, as if for the first time. Doing so will require discipline, a listening heart, and a great deal of honesty. In this book, we will limit our exposition to the Easter narrative, hoping that the following reflections will help us to get back in touch with the unrestrained joy of the original Easter proclamation and find its relevance for our daily lives.

PASSION AND DEATH

Trying to explain Jesus' resurrection by concocting a story that he never really died but somehow feigned death either through drugs or by substituting a look-alike for himself on the cross does not do justice to what little we do know about the events of Good Friday. Although the exact date is not known, most reputable historians agree that Jesus was condemned to death by Pontius Pilate, the Roman procurator of Palestine, and then tortured and summarily executed by his soldiers. It is also generally agreed that there was a certain degree of complicity in the action on the part of the Jewish high priest and Sanhedrin. For our present purposes, we are concerned only with the indisputable fact of Jesus' suffering and death on the cross and the effect his death had on his followers.

Many of his followers had seen in Jesus the victorious figure who would liberate Israel from its political domination and herald in a new age of peace. They could not understand Jesus' attempt to tell them otherwise. When he failed to meet their expectations, they reacted in a variety of ways. One of his closest followers betrayed him (Mk 14:43–46). Another denied he ever had anything to do with him (Mk 14:66–72). Most of the others simply ran away (Mk 14:50). But some remained faithful to him right to very end (Mk 15:40–41). They had loved Jesus very much and could not believe that his mission had ended in such dismal failure. Losing a loved one is difficult enough as it is; doing so in the midst of public shame and the breakdown of one's deepest hopes is even more excruciating. The events of Good Friday placed Jesus' disciples in a deep spiritual crisis. They were distraught, disillusioned, and afraid. Most of them had gone into hiding. It was to people like these that the Easter proclamation, "He is risen!" would first find the light of day.

THE RESURRECTION APPEARANCES

The tragic events of Good Friday gave way to the astonishing news of an empty tomb on Easter morning. The disappearance of Jesus' corpse from the sepulcher in which he was laid after his death came as a surprise to everyone. Even then, there were those who sought a rational explanation for this event. Matthew's Gospel tries to dispel rumors that the body was taken away by his followers by having the Jewish high priest go to Pilate and insist that he place a guard at the tomb to prevent such a scenario from ever taking place (Mt 27:62–66). The Easter proclamation, however, is not merely about an empty tomb, but about the disciples' actual experience of Jesus, their Lord and Master, whom they had presumed dead. Although the various Gospel accounts pertaining to these experiences are not historical in the strict sense of the term, they do contain a number of similarities. For example, when Jesus appeared to his disciples, he was not immediately recognized (Mk 16:12–13; Lk 24:13–35; Jn 20:11–18). This indicates that the resurrection was not merely a resuscitation of a corpse, but that Jesus was perceived differently, as living in some transfigured, glorified state. In any case, the Gospel accounts affirm that it was not merely Jesus' spirit or ghost that was experienced, but Jesus himself: body, soul, and spirit (for example, Jn 20:24–29). The underlying continuity between the earthly and glorified Jesus is a fundamental element of the Easter proclamation. All of who Jesus was on earth, in other words, continued to exist in a transformed state and was experienced by his disciples in the resurrection appearances. These experiences were given to a number of his disciples—both women and men—and in a variety of places. According to Paul, as many as five hundred of the disciples experienced the resurrected Jesus at one time (1 Cor 15:1–11). Just as startling as Jesus' appearances was the transformation that took place in the lives of those who saw him. This timid and fearful group of followers boldly proclaimed what they had seen and did so in the face of ridicule, persecution, and death. The amazing conviction of the disciples after the Easter appearances is the best evidence we have that their experience of Jesus was real. These men and women were not unbalanced religious fanatics who could be easily influenced by mood swings and what could be suggested to them simply by their deep desire to believe. They were practical people from all walks of life who knew who Jesus was and who testified with their lives that what they had seen was true.

THE ASCENSION

According to the Gospel of Luke and the Acts of the Apostles, Jesus appeared to his disciples over the course of forty days and then ascended into heaven (Lk 24:50–53; Acts 1:3). The writer of Mark, the earliest of the Gospels, says that Jesus "was taken up into heaven" after he revealed himself to the Eleven while they were at table (Mk 16:19). The two other Gospel accounts do not give a specific time when Jesus stopped appearing to them and took his seat at the right hand of the Father. Either they were not interested in determining a fixed time for when this occurred or (as is more likely) they wished to show its intrinsic relationship to the resurrection itself. Whatever the case, the ascension holds many important meanings. First, Jesus must leave his disciples in order to complete the redemptive action begun out of obedience to the Father's will. After his death and resurrection, it was only fitting that he should once again take up his proper place at the right hand of the Father. Second, the ascension underscores the transcendent character of the paschal mystery. In his transformed state, Jesus appeared to his disciples on a number of occasions and, according to the Gospel accounts, even ate with them (for example, Jn 21:1–12). He could do this because of the underlying continuity existing between his earthly and glorified states. At the same time, his kingdom was not of this world, but of the new creation that had been ushered in by his passion, death, and resurrection. The ascension is a theological way of saying that Jesus was no longer bound by the limitations of time and space. Because of him, we have been given a glimpse of that world and hope one day to journey to it. Finally, Jesus ascended to the right hand of the Father so that he could send us his Spirit and be present to us in a new way. Sporadic appearances in his glorified state to his disciples during the short period after his resurrection do not compare with the universal presence that becomes possible through the gift of the Spirit.

THE SENDING OF THE SPIRIT

According to the Acts of the Apostles, the Holy Spirit descends upon Jesus' disciples ten days after the Ascension. In Acts, the commissioning of the apostles and their sending out seem to be separate. The former is linked to Jesus' final words before his ascension (Acts 1:6–9), while the latter occurs ten days later on the feast of Pentecost when the Spirit manifests itself in tongues of fire and gives those who receive it the gift of tongues (Acts 2:1–13). In the Gospels of Matthew (Mt 28:16–20) and John (Jn 20:21–23), the gift of the Spirit is more closely connected with the resurrection appearances and the commissioning of the apostles. Whatever differences are noted in the Gospel accounts of the sending of the Spirit, this event is a direct result of Jesus' resurrection and ascension into heaven and a means of empowering the apostles to baptize, forgive sins, and preach the Good News with boldness and conviction.

The sending of the Spirit initiates the birth of the Church, the Body of Christ. The Spirit of Christ is the soul of this new, supernatural organism, while its believers form its many and diverse members. Through baptism, the Spirit immerses us in Christ's death and resurrection. In this ritual, Christ's redemptive action extends through space and time. Christ is the sacrament of God; the Church, the sacrament of Christ; the seven sacraments, those of the Church. The Holy Spirit is the point of continuity uniting each of these various dimensions of sacramental action. A sacrament is an outward sign of invisible grace only because the Holy Spirit makes it so. Another name for the Holy Spirit, in fact, is "Uncreated Grace." Whatever graces we receive either directly from God or through the visible signs of the sacraments themselves come to us only in and through the Spirit.

THE EUCHARIST

All of the various dimensions of the paschal mystery converge in the Eucharist which stands in obvious continuity with the long tradition of the Hebrew prophets. Hosea's marriage to the faithless Gomer (Hos 1:2–9), Jeremiah's symbols of the loincloth (Jer 13:1–11) and the shattered wine jugs (Jer 13:12–14), Ezekiel's making of bread from a single pot of wheat, barley, beans, lentils, millet, and spelt (Ezek 4:9) and his mime of the emigrant (Ezek 12:1–20) are all examples of the prophetic use of material signs and actions to convey the message of Yahweh to his people. These utterances of the Word of God actually bring into effect what they symbolize: God's word does not return in vain (Isa 55:11). In this respect, Jesus' breaking of the bread and drinking of the cup in the company of his disciples brings the reality of the paschal mystery into their midst. In other words, before his death, Jesus makes present the redemptive effects of Good Friday in the bread and wine which he eats and drinks with his disciples. These effects culminate in his Easter rising, his ascension, and his sending of the Spirit. Thus, the entire Christ event centers around the Eucharist. It makes present both the sacrifice of Calvary and the Risen Lord himself who, having ascended to the right hand of the Father, is present to the believing community through the gift of his Spirit and the transformation of bread and wine into his body and blood. It is for this reason that the Eucharist is considered the source and summit of the Church's life. It is also for this reason that we are encouraged to celebrate the sacrament frequently. Through the Eucharist, we are nourished by Christ himself and have the opportunity to be more deeply incorporated into his paschal mystery. Taking part in the Eucharist is the most intimate way to give thanks for the saving work accomplished for us in Christ.

THE RELEVANCE OF THE RESURRECTION

Our involved reflection on the main elements of the Easter narrative should have an immediate impact on our present life of faith. To discover this relevance, we need to look at each of the elements we have discussed previously to see how they impact on our religious outlook.

First, contemplating Jesus' suffering and death forces us to confront our attitudes toward failure. This part of the Easter narrative is one that many of us would rather overlook. We distance ourselves from Jesus' passion and death because the failure of the cross is in complete opposition to the narrative of "The American Dream" that deeply informs our consciousness. However, it is when we fail, not when we succeed, that our true character comes to the fore. At such moments, we discover what is most meaningful to us, what we really believe in; we get in touch with our deepest, truest self. It is from the midst of failure that we recognize our inner poverty and need to depend totally on the Lord. It is from the depths of defeat that we undergo an inner transformation and find the resilience of spirit that enables us to pick ourselves up and carry on. Our deeper, truer selves have ascended from the depths of our soul into the light of our conscious awareness. When this occurs, we become present to ourselves in a new way. We have become vital, spiritual persons who care not only for ourselves and others, but who cherish their relationship with God and to the world that God has placed us in. Everything we do becomes an opportunity for giving thanks to the Lord for his many gifts.

Each one of us goes through our own, very personal experiences of suffering, death, resurrection, ascension, spiritual renewal, and thanksgiving. These moments are not unrelated to the Christ event, but intimately a part of it. They remind us of the deepest realities of our lives and what penetrates the fabric of daily experience. They suggest that, even now, we are deeply involved in the mystery of the Christ event. They tell us that what we hope for is taking place in our lives at this very moment. They encourage us to peer into the depths of our experience and find there the drama of the paschal mystery in a very concrete way.

CONCLUSION

Christianity tells us that the death and resurrection of Jesus not only happened but is also taking place in us, the members of his body. However, many of us are unable to find a concrete link between the major elements of this Easter narrative and our daily experience. The Easter proclamation is the narrative of the new creation. It is the place where the book of creation and the book of the Word come together and ultimately merge. The point of this convergence is our own lives.

When we look within our hearts and ponder what we find there, we eventually come upon a faint but lasting reflection of Jesus' paschal mystery. In that reflection, we come to see that our present struggle between life and death has already taken place in the drama of the cross. That drama opens up to us a deeper dimension of life, one that we have never experienced before. Jesus' death on the cross reveals to us the power of love in our struggle against death. It shows us what lengths love is willing to go to for the renewal of the human heart. It tells us that the new creation of Spirit and Truth is inscribed in our hearts and will never die.

It will never die, because Jesus will not allow it. Belief in the Risen Lord comes from him in order to draw us gradually back to him. It keeps alive in us the hope that our lives will not end in death, but will merely change. It helps us to look forward to a transformed existence, one in continuity with our present lives. It encourages us to sustain a prayerful response to the contemporary challenges of Christian discipleship, especially at our celebration of the Eucharist. It forms the basis upon which life in the resurrection is anticipated in the present, thus enabling us to live each moment to the fullest.

Spiritual Exercise

Locate a Bible and read one of the Gospel accounts of Jesus' passion, death, and resurrection. As you do, note the various characters that Jesus meets along the way. Take note also of the various details of the account (for example, what happens to Jesus, what he says, to whom he appears after his resurrection). When you have finished, close your Bible and get some writing materials. Choose one of the characters in the Gospel narrative and, allowing your imagination to run free, compose an account of what happened to Jesus through this person's eyes. Try to enter into the person's thoughts and emotions. Write down not only what you think this person saw and said but also what he or she was thinking and feeling. Try to provide as many details as possible. If you do not feel like writing these reflections down on paper, then simply close your eyes and carry out the exercise in your mind.

When you have completed this part of the exercise, take another piece of paper and write down your own reactions to Jesus' passion, death, and resurrection. What impact, in other words, has the Gospel narrative had on your life? How has it affected your behavior? Do you have trouble believing it? If so, have you ever shared this difficulty with others? If not, have you ever shared your faith with others? Do you think about Jesus often? Do you pray to him? Do you share your feelings with him? Be honest with yourself—and be specific. What concrete evidence can you show that the Gospel message is important to you? Are there any other narratives in your life that compete with it? If so, can you identify them? Are you happy with them? Do you wish to change direction? If so, what can you do about it? Have you ever asked the Lord for help in doing so? Let these kinds of questions guide your reflection. Once again, if you do not feel inclined to write your thoughts down on paper, then simply reflect on your relationship to Jesus and his message.

Prayer

Lord, during this season of Easter proclamation, I praise you for your passage from death to life and ask you to gradually work the same transforming miracle in me. You have demonstrated, O Lord, that the power of love is stronger than death. Fill me with your love, Lord.

Help me to understand what it means to lay down my life for others. Teach me to be a servant. Help me to understand what it means to put others first. I look to you, Lord, to discern the way that I should walk. Help me to listen, Lord. Enable me to embrace the message of Easter morning with my whole heart, mind, and soul. Help me to see beyond the crosses that I must bear. Enable me to entrust my doubts to you and eventually to overcome them. Lead me to proclaim your message. Lord, I believe; help my unbelief. Give me the strength and the courage to walk in your footsteps. I love you, Lord. Help me to love you more.

CHAPTER SIX

COMPLETING THE CYCLE: CONTINUING THE SEASON OF ORDINARY TIME

Prayer, the Church's banquet, Angels' age,
God's breath in man returning to his birth,
The soul in paraphrase, heart in pilgrimage,
The Christian plummet, sounding
heaven and earth;
Engine against the Almighty, sinner's tower,
Reversed thunder, Christ-side-piercing spear,
The six days' world transposing in an hour,
A kind of tune, which all things hear and fear;
Softness, and peace, and joy, and love, and bliss,
Exalted manna, gladness of the best,
Heaven in ordinary, man well drest,
The milky way, the bird of Paradise,
Church-bells beyond the stars heard,
the soul's blood,
The land of spices; something understood.
GEORGE HERBERT, "PRAYER"[1]

A detail from Michelangelo's *The Last Judgment*

As the Easter season ends, Ordinary Time resumes, bringing the Church's liturgical year to a close. This second period of Ordinary Time focuses on the importance of the Christ event for the life of the believing community. It celebrates the presence of Christ's Spirit in the members of his body and looks to the fulfillment of the kingdom that is to come. This period of Ordinary Time not only ends the Church's liturgical year but also heralds in the new. It shares with Advent a deep concern for the eschatological (relating to the last things, that is, death, the Last Judgment, and so forth) nature of the Christ event and helps us to view all that happens to us with the eyes of faith. In doing so, it emphasizes the related nature of all the comings of Christ: to the world at Christmas, to the world at the end of time, and to depths of the human heart.

THE LAST JUDGMENT

One of the best metaphors for capturing the spirit of this second period of Ordinary Time is Michelangelo's *The Last Judgment* (executed between 1536–41). This famous fresco on the west wall of the Sistine Chapel in the Vatican Palace depicts the glorious Christ returning to the world at the end of time to judge the living and the dead. In it, the final skirmish of the cosmic battle between the forces of Christ and of Satan has taken place. With the defeat of Satan, the victorious Christ descends to the earth with his right arm raised in a decisive gesture. Everything in this scene revolves around Jesus' discerning motion, the overall effect of which is a heightened sense of drama and a visual sense in the eye of the beholder that the final judgment is actually taking place. Close around the Risen Christ are members of the faithful who are at various stages of their redemptive journey to God (that is, purgation, illumination, union). Farther below are those who have chosen to cut themselves off from the love of God. They have refused to repent; they have squandered their lives in the pursuit of false pleasures and now must live with the consequences.

For Michelangelo, the movement of history is building to its final point, one in which all that is hidden, including the deepest secrets of the human heart, will be revealed. At this decisive moment, the eternal destiny of each man, woman, and child will be made manifest. Some of the faces portrayed by Michelangelo on his fresco would have been familiar to his contemporaries, as if to say that the immediacy of this final judgment is at hand. His decision, moreover, to leave an imprint of his own face on the flayed skin of the martyr, Saint Bartholomew, is more than just an ingenious way of signing his work. It also tells us that no one—neither the beholder of this great masterpiece nor its creator—is exempt from Christ's pervasive justice—a justice that will not bestow forgiveness upon those who do not see their need for it and hence will not ask for it. Thus, each of us play an intimate role in our own judgment. At that moment, Christ will reveal to us the deepest truth about ourselves. He will show us the kind of people that we have become—either saved or lost.

Because it is in a chapel, Michelangelo's fresco reminds us of the essential role that prayer plays in helping to determine our destiny. Saint Alphonsus de Liguori (1696–1787) sums up this role in one sentence: "If you pray, you will be saved; if you do not pray, you will be certainly lost."[2] In a similar way, Ordinary Time gradually moves the community of the faithful away from the various seasons of the liturgical year toward a reflection on Christ's Second Coming at the end of time. During this season, the movement of the world toward its final consummation in Christ likewise dominates our thoughts. As we approach the final weeks of the liturgical year, we are reminded that, with each passing moment, we are getting that much closer to the end for which we were made. We are also reminded that prayer—liturgical and devotional, communal and private—is the great means of salvation. With it, we will slowly find our way to God and see him face to face; without it, we will close our eyes to the truth about ourselves and become increasingly lost in our own self-interests. For this reason, perseverance in prayer stands out as a major theme of the season.

ORDINARY TIME CONTINUED

Ordinary Time is considered a single season of the Church's liturgical year despite its interrupted observance. When we reflected on the spiritual meaning of first period of Ordinary Time, we adopted a past, present, and future focus. In this light, we discovered its strong connection to Jesus' ministry—his hidden life at Naza-reth, his Galilean ministry, and the events leading up to his passion and death in Jerusalem. We will use this same method for understanding the spiritual meaning that can be derived from the second period of Ordinary Time. We will look back, look around, and look forward.

LOOKING BACK

The second period of Ordinary Time resumes immedi-ately after the celebration of the feast of Pentecost, which represents the end of the Easter season and is commonly referred to as the birthday of the Church through which Christ's redemptive mission continues. With the sending of the Spirit to his apostles, Christ's followers are vivi-fied by his presence in their hearts and in their midst. It is the Spirit who works through the members of the Church to make God's love a concrete reality in every age and of every generation. Looking back on the Easter season from the perspective of this second period of Ordinary Time, we see that the Christ event is not con-fined to the events of Jesus' passion, death, and resur-rection, but has somehow extended itself beyond the boundaries of space and time. We understand that the paschal mystery is intimately bound up with the mys-tery of the Church and, as a result, with our own lives and deaths. A deep continuity exists between the Easter season and the second period of Ordinary Time. Christ's passion, death, and resurrection have brought a defini-tive change in the world. The old creation is gradually being reshaped into the new. The instrument of this re-creation is the Holy Spirit working through the members of Christ's body. If the first period of Ordinary Time highlighted the past, present, and future repercussions of Jesus' mission on earth, then the second period of this season focuses on the repercussions emanating from the public ministry of the Church. The Easter season passes the torch of Christ's redemptive action from the earthly Jesus to the Christ of faith whose Spirit vivifies the actions of his body, the Church. Seen as a unified season in the liturgical year, Ordinary Time strongly affirms the deep continuity between the Jesus of history and the Christ of faith. The second period of Ordinary moves our attention away from the historical ministry of Jesus to the ongoing mission of his body, the Church, of which we form an integral part. Our membership in the Church connects us with the ongoing redemptive mission of Christ and challenges us to dedicate our lives to discipleship and the work that such a life entails.

Discharging this role as a disciple requires answers to important questions. To what extent does belief in Christ's resurrection shape your outlook on life? Does it have any impact on your attitudes and values? Does it have any effect on the way you make your decisions? Would your life be any different without your belief in the resurrection? How does the Spirit fit into your understanding of what is important in life? Do you sense the Spirit's presence in your life? How does it vivify and motivate your actions? Does it give you a sense of mission? If so, how would you articulate it and how do you implement it in your daily life?

The answers to these questions bid us to examine the continuity between our beliefs and the actual way we live our lives. Do we allow the Spirit to permeate and vivify our lives, making the love of God visible in our own little corner of the world? Do we discharge our discipleship, not alone, but together as a family and in community? This is the challenge laid down by the second period of Ordinary Time: to live the life and undertake the responsibilities of the New Covenant formed as a result of Christ's paschal mystery, to recognize our movement through time as a newly created people destined to do great things for the love of God.

LOOKING AROUND

In this reflection on the second period of Ordinary Time, our focus turns to the Church's continuation of Christ's redemptive mission on earth, that is, to the sacraments. These visible signs of invisible grace are the mainstays of the Church's spiritual life, for they make present the saving action of Christ in the midst of the believing community. The seven sacraments are the actions of Christ in his body. In them, Word and symbol unite to become instruments of teaching, healing, and transformation in the life of the community and beyond. In the context of the second period of Ordinary Time, the sacraments are the primary means by which the Good News of Christ's redemptive action is proclaimed and realized in the world. Without them, Christ's presence in the world would be severely limited. With them, the members of Christ's body are nourished by the grace of the Spirit and enabled to carry on their mission of making the love of God manifest in the world.

This redemptive action is true of all seven sacraments, but especially of baptism, which makes us members of Christ's body and gives us access to the other sacraments, and also especially true of the Eucharist, which provides us with spiritual nourishment for our journey of faith. At baptism, we are incorporated into the paschal mystery of Christ—so much so that our lives cannot be fully understood apart from it. In the Eucharist, we gather around the table of the Lord to participate in a foreshadowing of the Messianic banquet, to commemorate and make present Jesus' sacrificial death on the cross, and to receive and eat the body and blood of the Lord himself. Banquet, sacrifice, and presence are the three primary characteristics of the Eucharist which, through the grace of God and the working of the Spirit, are meant to spill over into our lives. For this reason, we are called to celebrate and share with others, to give of ourselves, and to be incorporated more deeply into the love of Christ.

Our participation in sacramental life of the Church conforms our lives more deeply to the paschal mystery of Christ. As members of Christ's body, we seek to reveal the love of God to everyone we meet. We do this by immersing our lives in the life of Christ and his Church and by extending that life to others. There is a sacramental action appropriate for every stage of our lives from birth to death. In the light of the action of the sacraments, important questions arise. Do you take the sacramental teaching of the Church seriously? Do you really believe that at the moment of your baptism you were immersed in the passion, death, and resurrection of Jesus? Do you believe that the Eucharist brings you into the presence of Christ's sacrificial offering at Calvary, and gives you his body and blood as spiritual food? Have the sacraments become the mainstay of your spiritual life? Do you believe that, through them, the redemptive action of Christ gives all people the opportunity to hear the Good News and to respond to it according to their deepest desires? Do you believe that this redemptive action is bringing about a transformation in the world, turning the old creation into a new one based on the abiding love of Christ? Do you believe that time itself is a part of this gradual transformation and recapitulation of all things in Christ? Do you realize that every detail of your life can be offered to God and brought under the gentle sway of his redeeming grace? Are you persevering in your prayer? Do you bring the nitty-gritty details of your life to God? Do you lay them out before him and ask him to help you with your troubles?

LOOKING FORWARD

The second period of Ordinary Time gradually leads to the end of the liturgical year and to the beginning of the new one. On one hand, this period of Ordinary Time underscores the forward movement of history and its steady progression toward the final times. The readings toward the end of this part of the season are full of apocalyptic warnings of Christ's Second Coming and the imminent end of the world. On the other hand, this segment of Ordinary Time must also take into account the fact that no one knows precisely when the end will come and accept the probability that one year will simply lead into the next with little fanfare. It is at this point that the dichotomy of this season comes to the fore. As the liturgical year draws to a close, our hearts anticipate the approach of Advent. When it finally arrives, we find ourselves beginning the rhythm of the liturgical year all over again. How can we reconcile this seeming contradiction in the Church's celebration of the mystery of the Christ event? How do we reconcile this never-ending cycle of "ends and beginnings"? Rather than trying to attempt an explanation, our best response might be simply to recognize that at the end of each liturgical year something occurs close to what the mystics would call a "coincidence of opposites" (that is, the juxtaposition of contrary forces that reveal a deeper reality). The eschatological nature of human history, in other words, combined with our humble admission that we "know not the day or the hour" (Mt 25:13) moves us to commemorate the saving events of salvation history while they are still unfolding. From this point of view, *Chronos* (chronological time) appears as ongoing and cyclical, while from the point of view of *Kairos* (that is, sacred time), history is moving forward to its point of final consummation. The combination of the two in the Church's celebration of the liturgical year heightens the incarnational quality of the Christ event. Just as Jesus is the God-man, both human and divine, so too is his body, the Church. Just as Jesus was in the world, but not of it, so too is the believing community as it seeks to continue his redemptive mission through time. The commemorative nature of the liturgical year, however, memorializes the saving mysteries of the Christ event in a sacramental sense. In keeping with the sacramental nature of the Church itself, it effects what it signifies and enables believers not merely to remember, but actually to participate in the saving mysteries themselves.

Because our experience of this second period of Ordinary Time is, at one and the same time, both forward moving and cyclical, perhaps the composite metaphor of an upward spiraling action is the most appropriate way of describing what we are going through at this time of the liturgical year. Interestingly enough, this image of an upward spiral motion is one often associated with the threefold movement of purgation, illumination, and union so closely associated with growth in the spiritual life. Our journey toward God, in other words, often involves going through a series of purgative (relating to a cleansing that prepares a person for union with God), illuminative (relating to an inner transformation that makes God constantly present), and unitive (relating to a person's union with God) experiences that bring us forward, but not in a straightforward, linear manner. The upward spiraling motion combines a sense of the repetitive nature of the conversion process with the notion of forward motion or progress. By incorporating this movement into the dynamics of the liturgical year, we are reminded that our journey to God is not merely an individual venture, but one of an entire people. The Church itself is in constant need of conversion and must go through repeated phases of purgation, illumination, and union as well. Once more, these reflections on the second period of Ordinary Time trigger important questions. Do you feel as though you are making progress in the spiritual life? If so, has that progress been easy or difficult? What stands in the way? Do you ever feel as though you have been regressing? What does your life need to be purged of? What insights have you received about God's presence in your life? Do you think of your spiritual journey as being intimately tied to the Church's? Does the movement of the liturgical year reflect any of the rhythms that you yourself experience during the year? What have you done to participate in the Church's on-going redemptive mission? What can you do? The liturgical year in general and the second period of Ordinary Time in particular remind us that our lives are intimately bound up with the life of the Church and its historical mission. For this reason, we should live our lives as a reflection of the spiritual journey of the Church itself— and vice versa.

THE CALL TO URGENT LIVING

Looking back. Looking around. Looking forward. Using this approach to examining the second period of Ordinary Time, we uncover a "call to urgent living"—just as we uncovered a "call to simple living" in our examination of the first period of Ordinary Time. In the second period of Ordinary Time, we come face to face with our own mortality. Seeing that we have only one life to live and that we have no idea when our own final hour (or the world's, for that matter) will come, a sense of urgency to live our life the best way we know how gradually rises within our hearts. This call to urgent living is intimately related to the call to holiness. In this context, the words of Jesus take on special significance: "What profit would a man show if he were to gain the whole world and ruin himself in the process" (Mt 16:26). To gain the world means nothing if that world will one day come to an end. The second period of Ordinary Time reminds us that we must store up treasures in heaven. It also reminds us that where our treasure is, there also we will find our hearts (Mt 6:19–21).

This call is not a call to compulsive living. It does not mean busying ourselves with our work and leaving no time for our relationships with ourselves, others, and God. Living life with urgency does not mean fitting more and more into less and less increments of time. Nor does it mean abandoning our responsibilities in order to lose ourselves in pleasurable or other questionable pursuits, however worthy (even spiritual) they may appear to us at the time. It asks us only to allow God to accompany us in our daily tasks. It represents a quiet, constant call to conversion that resonates deep within our hearts and demands from us an unqualified response.

In practice, the call to urgency means that we take a good look inside our hearts and ask ourselves what matters most to us in life. Sometimes making a list can help us to see where our true priorities lie. When we finalize our list, and perhaps even in the process of writing it down, we may be surprised at what we find. We may say, for example, that God is very important to us, but discover that we fail to back up our words (and even our genuine intentions) with appropriate actions. In trying to do so, however, we inevitably find that we are incapable of giving ourselves to God without his assistance. Only when we open up to the Lord and humbly ask for his help do we eventually find the strength to turn our lives around and do what needs to be done.

So far, our description of the call to urgent living resembles what spiritual writers often refer to as the "purgative way." Identifying false priorities and attachments and freeing ourselves from them by cooperating with God's grace is an important part of the call to holiness—but is by no means enough. We also need a sense of where we are going. Direction is a very important part of the call to urgent living. We receive direction in our lives from many places. Parents and family, teachers and friends, figure greatly in the orientation our lives take. From the Church, we receive guidance through its teachings on faith and morals, by reading and meditating on its Scriptures, through our participation in its sacraments, and by praying with it as it moves through the various seasons of the liturgical year. We may also find personal prayer, shared prayer, group prayer, and talking with a trusted confessor and/or spiritual director helpful means for discerning what direction God wishes us to take in our walk of faith.

Receiving direction in our life of faith parallels what spiritual writers often refer to as the "illuminative way." This moment of the spiritual life gives us important insights into our relationship with God and points out for us the steps we need to take. It gives us a feel for the road we have set out upon and heightens our awareness of those with whom we are traveling, especially the Lord. For all its help, however, even this moment or stage of our spiritual journey does not suffice. The more we respond to the call to urgent living, the more insights we receive into our spiritual lives and the more our desire to walk the way of holiness deepens. In keeping with the second period of Ordinary Time, this call bids us to keep our end in sight and to make every effort to make our way there. We are all at different stages in our journey toward God. Wherever we are, however, all of us live in the hope of one day seeing God face to face. This hope draws us toward our final end (what spiritual writers often refer to as the "beatific vision," or the sublime and perfect knowledge of God that the person experiences after death) and enables us to persevere during difficult times. It further deepens our spiritual outlook and helps us to grow in intimacy with the Lord.

Living a life of deep personal intimacy with the Lord is not unlike what spiritual writers often refer to as the "unitive way." There are different degrees of intimacy, the deepest being what authors such as John of the Cross and Teresa of Ávila refer to as the "spiritual marriage," or the highest union with God. As hinted at earlier, however, it would be a mistake to think of the purgative, illuminative, and unitive ways as separate stages of spiritual progress that succeed one another in linear fashion without influencing one another in any way. A certain degree of intimacy with the Lord already exists as we travel along the purgative way. Moreover, even as we grow in intimacy with the Lord, we will still discover false attachments (perhaps some we had never seen before) of which we wish to be rid. If that is not enough, we will also receive new insights into our relationship with the Lord that will give further direction to our walk of faith. As we near the end of the liturgical year, this call to urgent living suddenly gives way to the gentle realization that God offers us plentiful redemption in Christ and that a deep spiritual marriage or union of souls is possible even for us.

CONCLUSION

The second period of Ordinary Time focuses our attention on the ongoing redemptive mission of Christ and our share in it as members of his body. As it nears its end, this season also focuses our attention on Christ's Second Coming, which completes the transformation of the whole world and heralds the fullness of the new creation. What we typically refer to as the "end of the world" is but a single facet of this ongoing process of transformation. We would do well to look upon our own deaths and the deaths of our loved ones in a similar vein.

During this season, we look back to the impact of the Risen Lord on our lives, we celebrate his sacramental action in the life of the Church, and we look forward to the transformation of the world into the new creation for which all of us so deeply hope.

The second period of Ordinary Time extends to each of us a call to urgent living. As members of the Church, we need to open our hearts and allow the Holy Spirit to purge us of whatever we have put in the way of our relationship with God. We also need to look for direction from those close to us and from the many means provided for us by the Word and worship of the Church. Most importantly, we need to do all we can to foster a deep, intimate relationship with the Lord. We only have one life to live and so little time to set things straight. The end of the liturgical year puts us in touch with the reality of our own earthly end. It challenges us to seize the moment and to do all we can to nurture in our hearts a deep love for God. This season reminds us that the world's end (and our own) is closer than we think.

Spiritual Exercise

Locate a full picture of Michelangelo's *The Last Judgment*. (A detail of this fresco appears on page 92 of this book.) Study it for a while. Notice how Christ is at the center of the dramatic scene of judgment. If you cannot find a complete picture of it, close your eyes and imagine by yourself what such a scene might be like. In either case, be sure to give Christ a central place in your mind's eye. Then place yourself in the picture and look at him. What does he look like? How does he seem? Do you see him as kind and merciful or as harsh and vengeful? What is he thinking? What is he saying to you? What are you thinking? What are you saying? Are you afraid of him? Are you ashamed to stand before him? Are you hiding anything from him? Are you asking anything of him? understanding? love? forgiveness? After you have placed yourself before the judgment seat of Christ in this way, open your eyes and continue to go about your daily life. As you do so, however, ask yourself if you ever think about your everyday life in the light of your future life. In other words, what impact does your knowledge of the end of your life have on the way you live your life now? Does keeping this end in sight help you along the way or distract you? Is it possible to think too much about the end? Too little? How does one find the right balance? Have you ever asked God to help you find it? Finally, do you know what the Church actually teaches about the last things? about the last judgment and the end of time? If not, are you curious enough to find out? If so, do you agree with it? Do you believe it will take place? Can you think of any other way of depicting it besides Michelangelo's version? besides your own?

Prayer

Lord, during this second period of the season of Ordinary Time, I ask you to help me to respond to the call to urgent living. Help me, first of all, to understand what this call means. Help me also to appreciate the many gifts you have given me. Let me not take anything for granted, not a single person or thing. As I look back on my life, I thank you, Lord, for the gift of the believing community. Thank you for your presence and continuing mission in your Church. Help me to revere this presence and to participate in the mission of your Church of which I am a member. Enable me to discover the particular contribution you wish me to make in it. As I look at my present circumstances, Lord, I am grateful for the gift of the sacraments. These enable me to nurture my relationship with you and to grow in the Spirit. Let them become an important part of my spiritual life. Inspire me to receive them often and to encourage others to do so as well. As I look to the future, I thank you, Lord, for the forward movement of time and for the transformation that will take place at its end. I also thank you for the movement of the seasons and the deep spiritual meaning that they impart. There is so much to be grateful for, Lord, and so much to look forward to. I love you, Lord. Help me to love you more.

NOTES

Introduction

1. These levels of spirituality come from Walter Principe, "Toward Defining Spirituality," *Studies in Religion/Sciences religieuses* 12 (1983): 135–36.
2. See *The Constitution on the Sacred Liturgy* in *Vatican Council II: The Conciliar and Post Conciliar Documents*, gen. ed. Austin Flannery (Northport, N.Y.: Costello Publishing Co., 1981), 1–40; Paul VI, *Apostolic Letter, Motu proprio: Approval of the General Norms for the Liturgical Year and the New General Roman Calendar*, in *The Roman Sacramentary* (New York: Catholic Book Publishing Co., 1974), 63–68; *Catechism of the Catholic Church*, nos 1168–73 (Vatican City: Libreria Editrice Vaticana, 1997), 303–4.
3. See, for example, Adolf Adam, *The Liturgical Year: Its History and Meaning After the Reform of the Liturgy*, trans. Matthew J. O'Connell (New York: Pueblo Publishing Co., 1981).

Chapter One

1. John Henry Newman, "Watching," sermon 22 in *Selection Adapted to the Seasons of the Ecclesiastical Year From the Parochial & Plain Sermons of John Henry Newman*, ed., W. J. Copeland (London: Rivingtons, 1878).
2. Samuel Beckett (1906–1989) first presented this tragi-comedy in French as *En Attendant Godot* (1952). He later translated and published it in English as *Waiting for Godot* (1954).
3. *De incarnatione*, 54.3 in *Sources chrétiennes*, vol. 199, ed. and trans. Charles Kannengiesser (Paris: Editions du Cerf, 1973), 458–59.
4. Seems to be an embellishment of the statement of Saint Alphonsus de Liguori: "The paradise of God, so to speak, is the heart of man." See *The Way to Converse with God* in *The Complete Works of Saint*

Alphonsus de Liguori, vol. 2, ed. Eugene Grimm (Brooklyn/St. Louis/ Toronto: Redemptorist Fathers, 1926), 395.

Chapter Two

1. John Milton, "On the Morning of Christ's Nativity" in *The Poetical Works of John Milton*, ed. Helen Darbishire (London: Oxford University Press, 1958), 395.
2. See Chapter 1, note 3.
3. *The Passion of the Infant Christ* (New York: Sheed & Ward, 1949), 61.
4 Ibid.
5. The following reflections depend on M. Helen Weier, *Festal Icons of the Lord* (Collegeville, Minn.: The Liturgical Press, 1977), 19–22.

Chapter Three

1. Henry Vaughan, "The World," *Great Poems of the English Language: An Anthology*, ed. Wallace Alvin Briggs with supplement by William Rose Benét (New York: Tudor Publishing Co., 1936), 234–35.

Chapter Four

1. Gerard Manley Hopkins, "Spring," *Victorian Poetry and Poetics*, eds. Walter E. Houghton and G. Robert Stange, 2d ed. (Boston: Houghton Mifflin Co., 1968), 700.
2. "The Acceptable Time," in *The Sunday Sermons of the Great Fathers*, vol. 2, *From the First Sunday in Lent to the Sunday After the Ascension*, ed. And trans. M. F. Toal (Chicago/London: Henry Regnery Co./ Longmans, Green, 1958), 13. For the original Latin of this sermon, see PL 17:636–37. Note: The original order reads: "…earnest in prayer and in almsgiving, in fasting and in watching."

Chapter Five

1. Alice Meynell, "Easter Night," in *The Poems of Alice Meynell* (New York: Charles Scribner's Sons: New York, 1928), 94.

Chapter Six

1. George Herbert, "Prayer," in *The New Oxford Book of English Verse: 1250–1950*, ed. Helen Gardner (New York/Oxford: Oxford University Press, 1972), 255–56.
2. *Prayer, The Great Means of Obtaining Salvation and All the Graces Which We Desire From God*, in *The Complete Works of Saint Alphonsus de Liguori*, vol. 3, ed. Eugene Grimm (Brooklyn/St. Louis/ Toronto: Redemptorist Fathers, 1927), 49.